A JOURNAL FOR COUPLES

Breathing Together

Cherish your Life by Breaking the Golden Cage of Emotions

ANUJA SAHOO

BLUEROSE PUBLISHERS
India | U.K.

Copyright © Anuja Sahoo 2024

All rights reserved by author. No part of this publication may be reproduced, stored in a retrieval system or transmitted in any form or by any means, electronic, mechanical, photocopying, recording or otherwise, without the prior permission of the author. Although every precaution has been taken to verify the accuracy of the information contained herein, the publisher assumes no responsibility for any errors or omissions. No liability is assumed for damages that may result from the use of information contained within.

BlueRose Publishers takes no responsibility for any damages, losses, or liabilities that may arise from the use or misuse of the information, products, or services provided in this publication.

For permissions requests or inquiries regarding this publication, please contact:

BLUEROSE PUBLISHERS
www.BlueRoseONE.com
info@bluerosepublishers.com
+91 8882 898 898
+4407342408967

ISBN: 978-93-5989-651-9

Cover design: Shivam
Typesetting: Namrata Saini

First Edition: January 2024

Contents

Preface v

Introduction 1

Chapter 1: GOLDEN CAGE OF EMOTIONS 5
    The formula for a Healthy Marriage: 14

Chapter 2: STRONG WOMEN MADE BY SCARS 17
    Kinds of Women Based on Personality: 22

Chapter 3: LEARNING LOVE IS A BEAUTIFUL THING . 27
    Her Techniques to Bring Life on Track: 36
    Her Mission to be a Respectable Woman: 39
    Her Husband's Changed Attitude - An
    Apology Message: 41
    Most Important Habits to Enhance Your Relationship: 42

Chapter 4: TOGETHER LIVE A GREAT LIFE 44
    Major Areas of Difference: 45
    Foundation of Marriage: 46
    Duties of Men in Family Life: Balancing Responsibilities
    and Expectations 50
    Good Qualities Expected: 52
    Duties of Women in Family Life: Nurturing, Prayer,
    and Support 53
    Qualities Expected of Women: 54
    Parental Duties: Nurturing Communication and
    Breaking the Cycle 55

Steps for Better Understanding between Parents and
Children:... 57

**Chapter 5: STOP MESSING WITH FUTURE
GENERATIONS** **64**

Role of mothers in a couple's life: 72
Story of a Joint Family: 73

Chapter 6: HEALING.. **78**

Navigate Your Life With the Purpose of Healing:............ 81
Both Partners Should Create An Image of a
Happy Family: 85
Build A Legacy for Your Family's Future:......................... 86
The Healing Process:... 88
Repeat these affirmations to cultivate a positive mindset
and influence your emotional well-being: 90

A Letter to the Reader

Dear Readers,

Wishing you all a joyful day filled with positivity and warmth. I extend my heartfelt gratitude to each one of you, and I sincerely hope you will bless me by reading this book until the very end.

In the pages that follow, I aim to share my thoughts and emotions about the world around us. Each chapter of this book is crafted with the intention of resonating with your lives, offering insights and reflections that may touch upon your personal experiences.

This book holds a special place for all couples who find themselves grappling with external and internal forces, endeavoring to bring their lives back on track. It is also a heartfelt gift for the incredible women navigating the delicate balance of relationships within their families.

At its core, this book delves into the intricate journey of married couples, exploring the challenges and pressures they face in their daily lives. It sheds light on how certain incidents can significantly impact their future, often in ways that may go unnoticed by parents and relatives. The narrative unfolds the shared struggles of both husbands and wives as they navigate the responsibilities, both new and old, that life throws their way.

Some are fortunate to receive the support of their families, while others may feel isolated in the unpredictable emotional cage. For those who resonate with this emotional turbulence, I believe this book has the power to transform your emotions and guide you toward becoming a better partner for your spouse. It has the potential to reshape aggressive and abusive relationships into ones filled with love.

In our present society, the sacred bond between husband and wife is facing challenges that pose a threat. This book is dedicated to nurturing healthy and thriving relationships between spouses. The profound significance of a strong marital relationship in shaping the emotional well-being and behavior of children is a central theme. A robust foundation of a loving marriage, I believe, can leave a powerful legacy that transcends time.

Family is undeniably the foundation of society, and marriage stands as the fundamental building block of the family structure. However, when marriages fail to cultivate healthy families, dysfunction can lead to emotional turmoil for children, resulting in long-term psychological and behavioral issues that strain the well-being and stability of society.

Nurturing strong and healthy families is a contribution to creating a harmonious and prosperous society.

"Our family and relationships live around us. Sometimes, they hold us together; sometimes, they split us apart."

Let's embark on a journey of connection through the pages of this book.

Thanks a lot,

Anuja

INTRODUCTION

> *"All the world's a stage, and all the men and women merely players."*
>
> - Shakespeare

Life and drama may seem similar, but there's a key difference. In drama, people follow a script, while in real life, we act based on our thoughts, beliefs, and the pressures around us. Ultimately, we're responsible for our actions and their outcomes.

We possess the power to shape our thoughts and create our reality. Being adaptable and willing to compromise for the well-being of our loved ones is crucial. Conflict is a natural part of any relationship, but resolving it in a healthy manner is important.

It's a fact that we all will face our end one day. Realizing that we won't live in this world forever can guide us to live a more meaningful life. This awareness prompts us to reflect on our actions. Just like when a child is born into a family, we begin to see the importance of making our time here count.

In those heartwarming moments, a beautiful sense of love and joy envelops the entire family. It's a time when even longstanding foes may set aside their differences, captivated by the pure innocence of the newborn. The child is surrounded by affection and positivity, fostering a deep sense of security and belonging.

However, as time unfolds, life's complexities start influencing the child. Different thoughts and vibes, whether from family or external sources, begin to shape the child's perspective. Some negative influences may gradually cast a shadow on the child's upbringing.

The most vulnerable stage of this transformation occurs during adolescence – a period marked by profound changes and heightened emotions. The impact of earlier negative influences may surface in destructive ways, affecting the adolescent's mental and emotional well-being. This can lead to behavioral and emotional struggles that prove challenging to overcome.

It serves as a reminder for parents and adults in the family to take profound responsibility, creating a positive environment and shielding them from chaos. It's about helping them navigate the turbulent thoughts of adolescence with resilience and strength. Achieving this requires every couple to balance their marriage and maintain a nurturing parenthood filled with love.

When a couple intertwines their lives with the promise of creating a promising future together, they often find themselves in a subtle dance of struggles and challenges beneath the surface of this shared dream. One of the most profound challenges faced by newlyweds is balancing their individual desires and expectations within the broader family dynamics.

The transition from being part of one generation to creating a new one can lead to tensions. Different expectations and unresolved issues can leave lasting scars on the newlywed relationship, giving rise to negative emotions that may impact their future together.

As the years pass and the couple ages, these scars can grow, becoming constant reminders of unhealed wounds from the past. When they become parents, these lingering emotions can hinder the enjoyment of parenthood. As parents of adolescents, they confront the harsh reality that the problems faced by their teens mirror their own neglected relationships. Their unsolved past acts as an unforgiving teacher, revealing that trivial disputes and misunderstandings cannot be easily undone.

It is in these moments of realization that parents comprehend the true value of balance in their relationship. They understand that their choices have a ripple effect through time, influencing not only their own lives but also those of their children and future generations. Recognizing this, they may strive to mend past wounds and create a more harmonious environment for themselves and their family.

In the intricate journey of a couple, the support of elders becomes crucial. Elders, drawing from their wisdom and experience, should offer strong support to newlywed couples. This support empowers them to navigate their unique path with greater clarity. Couples often grapple with finding a balance between personal aspirations and family obligations. Every choice they make today has a profound impact on shaping future generations.

The decisions and dynamics within a couple's relationship not only influence their destiny but also shape the destiny of the next generation. This book serves as a testament to the enduring power of love and understanding in constructing a harmonious life and leaving behind a legacy of happiness for generations to come.

A moving realization unfolds when a person sees their spouse as a teammate rather than an opponent. This shift is transformative, as together, they can construct a castle of happiness in their shared life journey.

The proper administration of a family structure is crucial. When it lacks effective management, it can lead to the emergence of individuals who pose a threat to both the family and society. Therefore, it's essential to create an atmosphere or environment that facilitates effective administration. This, in turn, helps in preparing responsible individuals who can actively contribute to the creation of a healthy and thriving society.

Chapter 1:

GOLDEN CAGE OF EMOTIONS

For every couple, the desire to enhance or heal their relationship is a common goal, yet achieving a better life together can be a challenging task. Numerous factors can impede their growth, leading to stress and unhappiness. The sensation of feeling overwhelmed is something both men and women may experience at various points in their lives. Men often feel it when shouldering significant responsibilities, while women may encounter it in response to the behavior of their husbands, in-laws, and children.

These feelings are universal experiences arising from the pressures individuals face in their relationships. Negative thoughts and emotions can create a sense of confinement within the duties we carry. Our perspectives on life, thoughts, beliefs, character, and life motivations no longer define us positively; instead, they can feel like chains limiting our individual freedom.

This is a crucial truth of life—a yearning for freedom to soar high, to reach for the sky of success and prosperity. Everyone is striving to break free from the old and embrace the new, to live life on their own terms.

But has anyone truly achieved everything they desired? Many people carry the weight of their unfulfilled wants in the world, often pondering what happiness and peace truly mean. There's a constant question of whether our thoughts are genuinely our own or mere reflections of what society has rooted in us. The influence of unseen forces and the grip of the past on our minds add to the complexities.

Sometimes, the conventional views of family and society hamper our individuality. When someone attempts to break free and create a new language of life, the pursuit of freedom can make them appear as a rebel to everyone. All must understand that true freedom isn't just about pleasure; it's about having the opportunity to do what is right for a better future.

In this journey, it's essential to disregard the opinions of those who may not be happy for you, recognizing that their discontent may stem from their own unhappiness. Taking control of one's thoughts leads to control over life. Achieving desired goals often requires drastic changes in our thoughts and actions.

Ultimately, the aim should be to become a comfortable person, someone with whom others feel at ease. It's a reminder that true freedom is not only about personal satisfaction but also about creating an environment where everyone can coexist comfortably.

Take the example of a dandelion, as it mirrors the emotional journey of human life. Just like a dandelion begins its journey as a tiny seed, we commence our lives with boundless innocence and promises. As it grows, the dandelion encounters various challenges, much like the ups and downs we face in our lives for emotional development.

In spring, the dandelion's bright yellow bloom represents the moments of joy and happiness in life, reminiscent of when a couple starts their journey together. These are times when emotions are vibrant, contentment is high, and dreams for the future are abundant. However, like dandelion petals that eventually wither and fall, these moments are fleeting, reminding us of the impermanence of emotional highs.

As the dandelion matures and transforms into its white, fluffy seed head, it symbolizes the growing complexities of our lives as we age. The seeds of the dandelion are carried away by the wind, representing how our emotional experiences spread and influence the world around us. Our emotions become intertwined with our relationships, impacting those close to us and leaving a lasting legacy for the next generation.

Just like dandelion seeds carried by the wind to unexpected places, sometimes we find ourselves in unexpected circumstances or with unexpected personalities, akin to the growth of a new plant in an unforeseen location. Life, like the journey of a dandelion, is filled with transformations and influences that shape our experiences and the world around us.

Life, much like the dandelion's emotional journey, reflects our struggles, resilience, and hope for a brighter future. Despite adverse conditions, we seek to find resilience and survive, understanding that emotions, struggles, successes, and failures are integral parts of our lives. Through life's changes, we strive to find beauty in every stage and meaning in every moment.

The "Golden Cage" condition refers to the feeling of being trapped or restricted by one's own emotions. It occurs when individuals find themselves in a seemingly comfortable situation that, in reality, hampers their emotional well-being. These emotions may stem from past trauma, social expectations, or self-doubt, leading to a cycle of negative thoughts, behaviors, or relationships that may seem secure but hinder personal growth and happiness.

Breaking free from this metaphorical cage involves recognizing and addressing these negative emotions. Understanding the root cause is essential for liberation, requiring self-awareness, mindfulness, self-care, and introspection. By taking these steps, individuals can gradually dismantle the emotional constraints that limit their potential for personal development and happiness.

To release ourselves from the golden cage of our thoughts, emotions, and stressful married life, we must focus on a few key factors:

- **Letting Go of the Past:**
    - Holding onto our past can create a blockage in life.
    - Living in the past, dwelling on regrets and sadness for past incidents can hinder future progress.
    - Recognize that the past cannot be changed, and overthinking about it may impede future growth.

- **Self-Reflection and Personal Growth:**
    - Acknowledge that the biggest threat to a successful and fulfilling life can be oneself.
    - Being authentic from day one is crucial. People can sense fake behavior, so embrace your natural attitude with your spouse.

- **Embracing Imperfections:**
    - Understand that nobody is perfect. Both partners may have flaws, and accepting imperfections is key to a healthy relationship.

- **Parental Influence on Relationships:**
    - Children learn from what they see and hear in their families. Married life is reflected in parental behavior.

- In dysfunctional families with emotionally unavailable parents, children may struggle to develop high self-esteem.

- **Impact of Environment on Mental Health:**
  - Lack of a healthy environment can affect the mental health of children.
  - Immature parental behavior can pose challenges for children to grow into adults with a strong sense of self-worth.

- **Managing Stress and Anxiety:**
  - Parents' mood disorders and abusive behaviors affect the next generation.
  - Stress, anxiety, and worry should not control one's life; seeking support is essential.

- **Empowerment and Independence:**
  - Manipulative attitudes within a marriage can transform a submissive partner into an independent and empowered individual, which all may not accept.

- **Avoiding Revengeful Behavior:**
  - In a complex environment, revengeful attitudes may not bring happiness but create difficulties for others in the family.
  - Anger and a desire for revenge can lead to destructive emotional blockages and depression.

- **Live in the Present:**
  - Understand the importance of living in the present, appreciating the current moment, and removing fears about the future.

- Express gratitude to the universe for the peaceful and happy moments you are currently experiencing.
- Many couples waste time dwelling on the past or worrying about the future.

- **Be Your Own Boss:**
  - Follow your instincts and live a life full of authenticity and brilliance.
  - Remember that nobody cares about your plans and successes as much as you do, so focus on doing things that bring you satisfaction and happiness.
  - Avoid unnecessary drama to portray a successful life; genuine actions speak louder.

- **Creative Problem-Solving:**
  - Be creative in solving relationship problems.
  - Find clarity in your mind and consider alternative methods to address issues rather than being stubborn in love with your current approach.

- **Surround Yourself with Positivity:**
  - Create your desired family environment by surrounding yourself with loving and supportive people who are genuinely happy to see you both as a happy couple.
  - Invest time and energy in the healthy development of your marriage, as it's the best gift you can give to your child.

- **Overcoming Fear:**
  - Use your intuitive power, especially for women, to manage life and emotions.
  - Face fears head-on, watch yourself grow stronger, and gain confidence.

- **Gratitude and Mindfulness:**
  - Reduce stress and anxiety through meditation and yoga.
  - Be grateful for your present life; cherish what you have and express gratitude for the things you currently possess.

- **Self-Reflection:**
  - Self-reflect on your emotions and understand the thoughts that lead to your emotions.
  - This self-awareness can help you navigate the limitations of your emotional cage.

- **Communication Breakdown:**
  - Emotional and personal blockages can lead to breakdowns in communication.
  - The inability to express feelings, needs, or concerns may create misunderstandings and conflicts.

- **Emotional Distance:**
  - Unresolved problems, past trauma, or negative thought patterns can create a lack of emotional intimacy.

- **Conflicts and Misunderstandings:**
  - Dealing with emotional issues may lead to reactions that partners don't understand, escalating disagreements.

After many years of unhappiness, Rima woke up one morning with a cloud of negative and depressive thoughts. As she reflected on her wedding day, she remembered the young woman who, captivated by her own beauty, presented herself as a perfect match, making a lasting impression on everyone, including her overwhelmed husband.

In the initial years of marriage, life began to unfold its changes. The arrival of a child brought new challenges, especially sleepless nights that seemed to stretch endlessly. While the rest of the family enjoyed sound sleep, her husband peacefully slumbered on the other side of the bed. In the first five years, Rima managed everything smoothly, always striving to provide comfort to her husband, who, in turn, was deeply engrossed in his work with little time to attend to her emotional needs.

With the birth of their second child, Rima found herself physically weakened, balancing the demands of motherhood and the toll it took on her well-being.

The husband seemed to lose his attention towards his wife, creating emotional turmoil in her mind. In the initial two years of their marriage, both had spent quality time together, with the wife focusing primarily on her husband's needs. However, when children entered their lives, Rima's attention shifted entirely to the upbringing of their offspring.

One day, as the husband returned home from the office, he found his wife disheveled, tired, in pain, and running a fever. Although he noticed her condition, he didn't inquire and went to another room for rest. This led Rima to feel ignored and frustrated, and eventually, she broke down in tears. When he finally approached her to ask what happened, she exploded with anger, expressing her grievances about his apparent indifference towards her.

At that moment, both of them erupted in anger, exchanging harsh words. Rima complained about how he didn't inquire about her well-being despite seeing her unwell, especially at odd times. The husband, unaware of her condition, also exploded with frustration. This exchange of anger and unmet expectations highlighted the growing emotional distance between them, emphasizing the need for open communication and understanding to bridge the gap in their relationship.

He stood at the door, ready to leave the house forever. Rima shouted, "Stop!" and fainted. When she came to her senses, she could only murmur, "Please, don't leave me alone now. I need you. I couldn't handle myself without you." Hearing the pain in his wife's voice, he felt a profound ache in his body and mind. The doctor diagnosed her with mental depression, revealing that she hadn't slept for at least the last three days. At that moment, he truly understood the depth of her suffering.

Until then, he had thought she was content with their children, believing she no longer cared for him. Now, a strong realization hit him – in the past seven years, he had left her alone to manage all the responsibilities of their relationship and children. Overwhelmed with guilt, he hesitated to approach her and admit his mistakes.

Sensing something amiss, she apologized and pleaded for him to come to her, expressing her need for his presence. She assured him that he didn't have to do anything; she just wanted to feel protected, to know that someone was there for her in times of pain, not just during moments of joy.

He walked over to her, held her hand, and sat quietly beside her. At that moment, he recognized a pattern in his behavior – he loved her back when she was happy but distanced himself and blamed her when she was unhappy. He realized that he had never asked why she was upset, and this awareness became a turning point in their relationship.

On that day, his feelings were different from any other day — a surge of real love and unconditional support for his wife. He reflected on the times when he fell ill, and she dedicated every minute to serving him, even neglecting her children on those days. Despite her selflessness, he had misunderstood her as a selfish woman.

Questioning himself, he wondered how she managed all these years in emotional imbalance without his help. He had always felt neglected, thinking he was the most overlooked person by his wife. He desired her to be energetic, happy, and in a good mood, capable of serving him well and assisting him in every aspect of life. It dawned on him that, in all these years, he had never truly looked at her directly, never sat with her, never inquired about her health. All she needed was his affectionate words, but he was mentally unaware of how to handle adverse situations in family life, leading to his unloving and indifferent behavior towards her.

That day marked a turning point as he discovered a new way to improve their relationship. He realized that couples often face problems due to a lack of awareness that women and men are different in some aspects. Men may become angry and frustrated with their wives, assuming they think and react the same way. Women, while independent, need soft and loving words to heal from stress. The expectations placed on each other lead to misunderstandings, making relationships challenging. Awareness of these differences and embracing effective communication can pave the way for a more harmonious connection.

THE FORMULA FOR A HEALTHY MARRIAGE:

To start and maintain a happy family, there are some principles elaborated in Chapter Four. Here are basic habits essential for a joyful life:

- **Effective Communication:**
  - Learn ways to communicate during difficult times, such as through letters, emails, or messages.

- This helps in creating a healthy and forgiving relationship.

- **Avoiding Painful Arguments:**
  - Men shouldn't act as if they are always right.
  - Women should learn the best times for conversations with their husbands.
  - Men need acceptance and unconditional trust, while women need understanding, respect, and a friend who listens without offering solutions.

- **Open and Honest Communication:**
  - Addressing problems requires empathy and open, honest communication.

- **Expressing Emotion Creatively:**
  - Use creative expressions like writing, music, or voice messages to convey emotions, providing a sense of freedom for communication.

- **Body Language:**
  - Use soft, kind gestures and peaceful facial expressions to express positive emotions toward your spouse.

- **Emotional Well-being:**
  - Everyone's emotional journey is unique, so self-care and support are crucial to address emotional turmoil.
  - Engage in activities that promote emotional well-being and find healthy ways to express feelings.

- **Mindfulness and Relaxation:**
    - Practices like yoga, meditation, and deep breathing increase self-awareness and help manage emotional turmoil.

- **Build a Support System:**
    - Connect with supportive friends and family who understand and validate your feelings.

- **Avoid Toxic Habits:**
    - Don't make your partner feel ignored or unwanted.
    - Avoid purposely replying late to make them miss you; it's a toxic habit that should be avoided.

- **Start the Day Together:**
    - Every morning, have tea or coffee together and engage in a nice conversation to start the day positively.

Remember, every marriage is different, and every couple is unique. Embrace and adjust to differences, fostering a beautiful and harmonious relationship.

Chapter 2:

STRONG WOMEN MADE BY SCARS

"She is humble but strong. She is gentle but hates dishonesty. She is giving but not naive. She is adorned with dignity but chooses not to show pride. She has everything but chooses not to flaunt."

Every woman possesses unique powers and qualities through which, in the grand tapestry of life, she contributes to the growth of civilization. It's essential to recognize and appreciate the diversity of roles that women play—whether as housewives or working professionals. Each role comes with its distinct set of challenges and ways of handling problems, and both are equally respectable.

In the upcoming chapters, we will delve into real-life stories that showcase the different perspectives and strengths women bring to various aspects of life.

This book serves as a guide for all couples, with a special focus on empowering women. It is designed to help you harness your strengths and promote your power, leading to a more comfortable and fulfilling life in every aspect.

A woman is like a magical wand; you can't truly comprehend her strength until she's alone and struggling. This speaks to her inherent quality of adaptability, the tradition of her transitioning to her husband's house after marriage being a testament to this strength. God has endowed her with resilience, enabling her to give birth, raise children, and support the family despite facing numerous health challenges.

Yet, despite her evident strength, a woman can be vulnerable in her relationship with her husband. She seeks security, loyalty, protection, and trust from her life partner. Unfortunately, some individuals may take advantage of this vulnerability. Strong women often choose to hide their vulnerability from others because they recognize the lack of proper support.

In instances where a woman apologizes for her mistakes, a husband should embody the role of a forgiving father, offering protection and guidance as he would for his own daughter. It is crucial for husbands to shield their wives from emotional attacks and provide support in finding balance and managing challenges.

A woman doesn't force you into doing things for her; instead, she supports you in your struggles and stands with you through both good and bad times. It's essential for a man to understand her emotions and never take her love and dedication for granted. Mind games and emotional torture should never be a part of the relationship. She is not a weak person; she sees her husband as a mentor, best friend, protector, and much more.

Upon entering marriage, a woman puts in her utmost effort to be a better wife. She treats her husband's parents with the utmost respect, aiming to maintain healthy relationships. However, despite all her efforts, questions linger. Why does she sometimes become the scapegoat in her in-laws' eyes? Why isn't her contribution to her husband's life recognized? Answers to these questions will unfold in the coming chapters.

As a woman, she consistently struggles to hold onto her life, gripping onto her relationship with her husband tightly, as if her very breath depended on it. There are moments when she feels breathless, losing faith in her husband. During these times, she finds strength through patience and trust, regaining her power of intuition. She comes to understand that her primary relationship is with herself, and she begins cultivating a loving relationship with her own feelings. Creating a forgiving space becomes crucial, enabling her to unleash her power and reclaim her sense of self.

Every woman should embrace mental toughness and spiritual trust, essential elements in creating a better home.

Here's a motivational quote by A.P.J Abdul Kalam:

> "The essence of a happy life and a peaceful society lies in one sentence - What can I give?"

Instead of blaming your spouse, focus on self-empowerment and personal growth. Take responsibility for your past, present, and future. Empowerment comes from within, and taking control of your life is your responsibility. This shift in mindset will free you from negative emotions and fuel positive ones.

In the grand tapestry of the universe, everything happens for a reason. It might take time to realize the effects, but finding the reasons behind changes in your life is crucial. Ask yourself, what does your heart desire to achieve? Organize your life by analyzing your past—acknowledge mistakes and understand how you behaved under pressure. Envision yourself as an outstanding woman, empowered in every aspect of your life.

In challenging situations, consider how you would like to behave and value yourself. Hold onto your dreams and hope for the best in life, as these aspirations will help you stand tall.

Many women have faced difficulties in the past, falling into the trap of tough times and wrong people. It's important to let go of the past; your past is not your future. Instead of dwelling on regrets, focus on shaping a positive future.

The role of women is not solely defined by financial independence; true empowerment comes from empowering thoughts. Even without financial independence, women can feel empowered by nurturing their families. They protect their children from negative influences, prioritize their family, and rely on their natural instincts for effective child-rearing. The contribution of a non-working woman to her family and community is no less significant than that of a working woman. Remember, a happy woman makes a happy home.

You have an enemy inside you, and that's your thoughts. Tame them so you can fight for your well-being.

Women can empower themselves by acquiring knowledge and developing various skills, finding success and fulfillment in life.

Don't Be Too Much Loving - Not everyone will have the heart you have. Some will appreciate you and what you do for them, while others may not. It won't always be easy having a kind heart in a cruel world, so be prepared for it.

Be your own cheerleader, maintaining a positive mindset to appreciate yourself. Every young girl dreams of marrying and establishing a family, but the reality of married life can be challenging. It's essential not to let negative comments from others, especially those with a pessimistic mindset, influence your perception. Not all marriages face difficulties, and it's crucial to focus on positive examples.

During the early years of marriage, some women may feel the need to please others and undertake chores outside their comfort zones, leading to challenging situations. However, this isn't the case for every woman. Some are living fairy-tale lives, prioritizing their own needs. This isn't a bad thing, especially for financially independent women who can take care of their happiness without depending on others.

Earning women often face different attitudes from family members who may expect and sometimes demand honor due to their sense of self-value. Despite the lack of acknowledgment, a housewife tends to be more loving towards her husband and family members. Even in the face of neglect, she plays the role of the family's queen, handling problems with patience and standing alone when she loses her temper. Despite misunderstandings, she chooses to honor her husband and stands behind him, protecting him from negativity. She recognizes her power, is blessed by divinity, and trains her heart and mind, hoping for a beautiful and perfect life in the future.

Every woman desires respect and freedom to breathe with peace. Being overly loving and caring can sometimes reveal vulnerability. Loving and caring women often bear a unique burden, as their emotional nature makes them susceptible to suffering. Their tenderness can become a double-edged sword as they absorb the joys and sorrows of those around them. This deep emotional connection may lead them to suffer profoundly, forgetting their own existence in the process.

Every woman should embrace the process of self-discovery that helps her become her best version. Self-love, at times, is not selfish; it involves focusing on oneself and developing the strength to balance different qualities.

KINDS OF WOMEN BASED ON PERSONALITY:

Find out what type of woman you are or the type of woman she is:

1. **Queen:** Confident, self-motivated, ambitious, and passionate, with a strong sense of self-love.
2. **Kindest Angel:** Mostly forgiving, shows motherly love and care, is empathetic, and displays respect for everyone.
3. **Divine Woman:** Graceful and composed, rooted in gratitude as a central aspect of her life.
4. **Warrior Princess:** Stands up for herself and others, believes in trust and justice, shows courage without fear, and sets boundaries for self-protection.

All women have different personalities, and none is bad in her place. Each possesses these qualities in varying proportions. Accepting a woman as she is, with her unique personality, is essential. Your personality reflects who you are, and understanding and appreciating these differences can lead to stronger connections.

In the first case, a woman with a Queen personality takes on leadership and responsibilities within her family. She plays a crucial role in decision-making and guiding her family, ensuring the well-being of her family and children. Actively participating in the community, she contributes to building and supporting those in need. With a strong work ethic, she passes down traditions, values, and knowledge to the next generation, displaying excellent communication skills.

In the second case, the kindest and most loving woman is known for her angelic, loving, empathetic, respectful, and generous attitude. Her heart is as big as the sky, and her smile can light up even the darkest of days. Her boundless love extends to everyone around her, and her empathy allows her to understand the pain and joy of others. She treats every person with respect, and generosity flows from her like a river. She envisions a world filled with love and actively contributes to creating that reality.

In the third case, the Divine Feminine woman radiates an aura of composure and grace, enchanting everyone who crosses her path. She demonstrates unwavering gratitude for the beauty of life, starting each day with a silent prayer before the sun's rays touch the Earth. Her thoughts drift gently, much like the softest of winds. Living a life devoted to faith, hope, and gratitude, these women serve as a source of inspiration, reminding others that amidst a chaotic life, one can find serenity. Their lives flourish by embodying the qualities of grace, gratitude, and devotion.

In the fourth case, the warrior women have a spirit that dares to challenge difficulties. They embrace the ideology that apologies are accepted, but trust is not given lightly. Their approach to success is unique, as they don't fear admitting mistakes and offering sincere apologies. They firmly believe that trust should be earned and not freely handed out. Bold and unapologetic, they don't hesitate to distance themselves from those who cannot earn trust, considering trust as a valuable treasure. Committed to their principles, they refuse to compromise on trust.

Every woman possesses a blend of strength and vulnerability, and within each woman, all four personalities exist in varying proportions. Some embody the grace of authority, others endless empathy and compassion, some spirituality with inner peace, and some are fearless and strong. Despite the varying proportions, women stand strong in the face of adversities, displaying a combination of these qualities.

Life may not always be fair, presenting challenging tasks that require the best solutions to distinguish winners from losers. In adverse situations, those who reject being ruled by fear and negativity become warrior princesses, demonstrating courage, love, and faith, acting as survivors. It's essential to be stronger than what one might think about oneself. The inner thoughts and beliefs about oneself reflect in the outer world. Self-discipline is a source of strength that can be cultivated to navigate through challenges.

Walking on faith can bring numerous benefits and positive outcomes in a woman's life:

1. **Inner Strength:** Faith provides a sense of inner strength, enabling individuals to face challenges with resilience.
2. **Peace of Mind:** Guided and supported by faith, individuals can achieve peace of mind, even in the midst of difficulties.
3. **Courage:** Faith fosters courage, empowering individuals to confront and navigate through difficult situations.
4. **Empowerment:** Having faith can empower individuals to make decisions and choices confidently.
5. **Hope for the Future:** Faith instills hope for a better future and belief in positive outcomes.
6. **Purpose and Direction:** Faith can provide a sense of purpose and direction in life, guiding individuals on their journey.
7. **Acts of Kindness:** Grounded in faith, individuals may be inspired to perform acts of kindness and compassion toward others.
8. **Personal Growth:** Walking on faith often leads to personal growth and self-discovery.

9. **Fulfillment:** Ultimately, walking on faith can bring a profound sense of fulfillment and contentment.

Faith serves as a powerful motivating force that guides individuals in various aspects of their lives, influencing their decisions, actions, and overall outlook.

Maintaining a positive attitude can serve as a powerful source of motivation and contribute to overall well-being. Here are some key points about the importance of a positive attitude:

1. **Belief in Yourself:** A positive attitude involves believing in yourself and your abilities. This self-confidence can be a driving force behind taking on challenges.
2. **Reflection of Mindset:** Your attitude is a reflection of your mindset. Cultivating an optimistic mindset can influence how you approach various aspects of life.
3. **Problem-Solving Mindset:** With a positive attitude, you are more likely to approach challenges with a problem-solving mindset. This can lead to finding constructive solutions rather than dwelling on problems.
4. **Impact on Health:** A positive attitude can have a positive impact on both physical and mental health. It is associated with lower stress levels and improved overall well-being.
5. **Flexibility and Happiness:** Maintaining a flexible attitude, especially one that focuses on the positive aspects of life, contributes to greater happiness. Embracing optimism can lead to a more fulfilling and enjoyable life journey.

In summary, a positive attitude can be a catalyst for personal growth, resilience, and a more joyful approach to life's ups and downs.

Our emotions often influence our actions, and cultivating a positive attitude is key to shaping a better future. Strong and confident individuals have a clear vision of their beliefs, ideas, and future aspirations. The alignment between one's thoughts and actions is crucial for personal growth.

A positive self-image and envisioning a positive future can be transformative. The power of thoughts and internal dialogue plays a significant role in shaping our lives. It's important to engage in self-talk that reinforces positive qualities and aspirations. For instance, repeating affirmations like "I am a good, honest, truthful, hardworking, and responsible person" can gradually shape your self-perception.

These self-affirmations will not change you from day one. But upon practicing with full commitment, you will witness a drastic change in what you will be from what you are today.

Unconditional self-acceptance is a powerful tool. By acknowledging and accepting your strengths and responsibilities, you pave the way for positive change. Thoughts have the potential to transform into reality, and changing your internal dialogue can indeed change your life.

In relationships, including with a spouse, changing your thoughts about the person can positively impact the dynamics. Expressing love, appreciation, forgiveness, and gratitude can attract positive energy and events into your life. Conversely, negative thoughts, gossip, and assumptions can lead to adverse circumstances. Fostering a positive mindset within the family can contribute to building strong and harmonious relationships.

Chapter 3:

LEARNING LOVE IS A BEAUTIFUL THING

The journey of loving others is like a beautiful dance of emotions, weaving different patterns throughout our lives. We're all students, and love is our greatest teacher. It gently whispers its lessons through actions, words, and the unspoken gestures of those around us. Love doesn't come with a manual; it's not something we're explicitly taught. When we observe the world, we see some people filled with hope, others driven by greed, and some who fake love.

Learning how to give and receive feelings and emotions and how to build and nurture relationships is not part of our formal education. Our family and friends are also navigating this beautiful journey, exploring hidden and complicated paths in the mysterious forest of relationships. We witness the delicate balance of vulnerability and strength that love demands between husbands and wives.

Love isn't just grand gestures and declarations; it's also found in moments of care and kindness. It's the warmth of a hug, the sincerity of a smile, and the comfort of shared silence. Love isn't about perfection; it's about acceptance, forgiveness, and growth. Let it inspire us to become better versions of ourselves. Love isn't a destination; it's a journey guided by the wisdom of our hearts.

When we first meet our spouse, we strive to make our relationship loving and respectful. Initially, everything seems to be going well. However, after one or two years, life starts to reveal its true colors.

Here, I'm sharing the genuine challenges of relationships. Nowadays, many young people are hesitant to get married. The fear of handling marriage is widespread, and a significant number end up divorcing after a few years. A successful married life requires considerable support to thrive, akin to managing a project. If you're married and have children, it's like a 20-year project aimed at building well-being for your family.

For this project to succeed, both partners need to be on the right track with good communication and understanding. Otherwise, both may face struggles throughout their lives. We are well aware of the importance of marriage in society and the values it adds to our history.

Being in a marriage, especially for a woman, demands strength. The happiness of children is closely tied to the happiness of the mother. Children prefer seeing their parents as a united front rather than viewing them as separate individuals. They learn about relationships early in life by observing how their parents treat each other. Therefore, it's crucial for parents to laugh together, compliment each other, and, most importantly, respect each other.

Managing a successful and harmonious married life while upholding a healthy family legacy is indeed a complex journey for every man and woman.

In my neighborhood, there's a family that evokes both admiration and curiosity. Upon observing them, I noticed a whirlwind of dynamics within their relationships. The father, an underpaid employee, carries the weight of supporting his wife and four children on his shoulders, a responsibility clearly etched on his face. Despite financial challenges, he harbors ambitious dreams for his four vibrant and studious children, who are the pride of his life.

The mother of the family, a woman of boundless chatter, consistently sings praises for her husband and children. Her devotion to her family is evident in every gesture she makes. She takes pride in portraying her husband as a highly learned and knowledgeable person, presenting their relationship as an ideal one. At times, she tends to exaggerate about her family, making it a bit hard to believe. Nevertheless, she embodies the essence of a devoted wife.

I've witnessed her unwavering spirituality and the depth of her dedication to her husband. She wears her love for him like a promise, a commitment to honor and cherish him through thick and thin.

One day, I stumbled upon a scene that shattered my belief in the sanity of their marriage. I found her, breathless and in tears, confiding in my Aunt. When I asked what had happened, her revelation shocked me to the core. She hadn't eaten for three days because her husband, upset about some issues, had refused to eat for the same duration. To my surprise, my uncle overheard this and disclosed that he had seen her husband dining at a restaurant for lunch. I couldn't fathom how a man could enjoy a meal while his wife was starving and waiting for him for three days.

This incident, however, was not a one-time occurrence but a recurring pattern happening every month. Her husband's indifferent attitude cast a shadow of neglect and disrespect in their marriage, a hidden truth behind closed doors. Despite this, she clung to a fragile hope that one day, her husband would undergo a transformation, shedding his anger and embracing a more peaceful life. Her belief in the power of love led her to try to resolve the issue after enduring hunger for a few days.

She initiated efforts to balance their relationship, often expressing her pain through silent tears in front of her husband. Slowly, her husband's heart would return to normal. Their children found themselves caught in the stormy crossfire of this complex relationship. They learned to adapt, navigating the stormy seas of their household. Some withdrew from the emotional turbulence, creating their own worlds, while others sought refuge in academics and friendships outside the home.

The question lingered in my mind: What kind of relationship was this? It seemed like a blend of love and suffering, a constant battle between hope and despair.

The children carried the scars of witnessing their parents' complex relationship. They were left confused about their parents' attitudes toward each other, growing up with an understanding of the intricacies and complexities of human relationships. They learned that love could be a double-edged sword, capable of both healing and hurting.

The dysfunctional legacy of the family appeared poised to repeat itself as the elder son embarked on his journey with his wife. The relationship between his parents cast a haunting reflection on their marriage, and the same patterns began to resurface.

It's often the case that when childhood experiences are painful, we unconsciously strive to recreate similar situations throughout our lives.

The elder daughter-in-law is known for her loving and caring attitude, but beneath the surface lies a history rooted in a dysfunctional family. In her past, feelings and emotions were largely ignored, with her parents constantly fighting. This left her confused, often blaming her mother for her father's bad moods. In a household absorbed in its own problems, she found herself hungry for love and attention.

Coming from such an environment, girls in these families often yearn for love and attention, while boys may develop anger and destructive tendencies. Male children might become emotionally distant, selfish, and irresponsible, leading to unstable relationships in the long term.

The first daughter-in-law harbors a dream of a happy family. To achieve this, she starts doing things to please her husband and other family members. Her main hope is to receive love, respect, and a peaceful life. However, she becomes so absorbed in her relationship that her true creative mind struggles to function. In a way, she transforms into a robot, with the remote control held by someone else.

Her dreams revolve around finding a partner who values her emotions wanting to establish in her own life what she wished for in her parents' relationship. Paradoxically, she ends up manifesting a partner with an unhealthy mindset and an unloving attitude.

She never withheld her love; instead, she poured even more dedication into her relationship with her husband and in-laws. Research suggests that when a woman faces neglect in a marriage that doesn't meet her needs, she tends to become insecure. In response, she starts loving and caring more, driven by the fear of losing the relationship. This behavior becomes somewhat of an addiction for her and inadvertently satisfies her husband's ego. What she receives in return may appear as love, but he begins taking it for granted, becoming careless in his attitude toward her. In his mind, she becomes perceived as weak and vulnerable.

The fear of abandonment intensifies her efforts to be more loving and caring, turning her into a caretaker for her husband. Unfortunately, he doesn't recognize her as a wife but merely as a caretaker. Mirroring her mother-in-law's experiences, she falls into the same pattern of her father-in-law's old anger issues and her husband's current anger issues, creating an unhappy and unhealthy family environment.

Her routine includes fasting for her father-in-law's mood swings and then fasting again for her husband's anger issues. This family drama results in her spending several days without food. After about a year of this, something drastic occurs. She finds herself admitted to the hospital for a week, mirroring the behavior and emotional distress of her mother-in-law. The severe malnutrition and psychological stress become evident consequences of the family dynamics she's entangled in.

She shoulders all responsibilities with guilt and blame, not just assuming them but being compelled to accept them by her husband and in-laws. Deep down, she harbors the belief that she doesn't deserve to be happy. Silently, she endures the weight of familial expectations and emotional turmoil.

After being discharged from the hospital, a significant change is noticed in her attitude. She loses all interest in living, realizing that she had invested so much energy in the hope of receiving caring behavior from her husband. Now, she comprehends her mother's responses to her father, understanding that she has become like her mother. The enthusiasm to serve other family members with love diminishes, and she loses hope in her husband and in-laws. While she was once seen as a good daughter-in-law, she transforms into a perceived "bad character" for every family member.

However, a shift is observed when the second son enters into marriage with a woman of remarkable strength and unwavering values. She, too, finds herself entangled in the recurring patterns of the family. The second son is slightly different from the first, recognizing the financial independence and education of his wife. In their first year of marriage, a peaceful atmosphere prevails as they communicate openly without fear or hesitation.

The mother-in-law is uneasy about the second daughter-in-law's freedom. An unhealed woman struggles to see another woman happy, especially when she never enjoyed such freedom. Unable to embrace the changes in her son and daughter-in-law's lives, she imposes her own past on them, insisting that her daughter-in-law live lives similar to hers.

A man's mother plays several crucial roles in his life, being the first woman he encounters. He often expects the same respect and dedication from his wife as he has witnessed between his parents. Consequently, he may treat his wife similarly to how his father treated his mother, anticipating that his wife will feel obligated to follow the same patterns. This sometimes leads to controlling behavior, using anger as a means of control, mirroring the father's actions.

However, the daughter-in-law is different from her mother-in-law and sister-in-law. She is fully aware of the situation and understands why changes have occurred in her relationship. Growing up in an environment where men disrespect women, the man may unconsciously try to recreate a similar chaos in his married life. This leaves many women wondering with frustration, "What does he expect from me? I'm doing my best, but why isn't he happy?"

The mother-in-law influences her husband to be like his father, whom he considers an ideal man. However, the mother-in-law, carrying internal wounds, seems to desire that other women should experience the same pain and life drama she went through.

In this dramatic scenario, everyone becomes a team against the daughter-in-law. On one side, there's her husband, his parents, sisters, and brother. On the other, she finds herself alone in the fight against the situation, with only her elder sister-in-law showing some empathy.

Pain has a transformative effect on people, and it changes her loving attitude toward her husband. When a man feels defeated in manipulating his wife, he may resort to targeting her character and exacerbating the situation. Matters worsen, leading her to consider divorce. However, deep down, she doesn't truly desire separation. This realization also impacts her husband, who starts to understand the sensitivity of the matter.

Marriage is a complex journey between two people, where both expect love, support, and trust from each other. The emotional value that fulfills a marriage is equal for every couple. A solid foundation is necessary to withstand any storms in life. The second daughter-in-law shares a strong emotional bond with her husband. In the first year of their marriage, they enjoy a healthy marital life with good communication. However, when she starts living with her in-laws, issues between the two couples in the family begin to affect her. Her complaints and opinions about these matters create problems in her life.

She was a remarkably beautiful, gentle, and smart girl, and the couple looked great together. However, when she lived with her in-laws, her vibrant charm diminished, and she became lean and thin. As a daughter-in-law, she refrained from eating if other family members were fasting due to her father-in-law's influence. Her mother-in-law expected her to follow suit, and when she complained to her husband, he avoided the conversation, lacking the courage to confront his parents and unsure how to resolve the issue.

The husband began blaming her, asserting that she wasn't accepting his parents as her own, leading to misunderstandings. This communication breakdown escalated, and the husband stopped talking to her. When she called, he didn't respond, responding eventually with a complaint that she never understood his feelings and how lonely he felt.

She recognized that her husband was following the same pattern as she had witnessed in the behavior of the other two male family members toward their wives. Despite education and intelligence, the deeply ingrained behavioral patterns of the family remained unchanged.

This situation serves as a reminder that, although love is a powerful force, it isn't always enough to mend the deep-seated wounds beneath one's heart.

One day, she opened up to her close friend about all her emotions and received guidance not to lose patience. She started reading different motivational books, and in one of them, she came across a paragraph that struck a chord with her:

"Your life's greatest storm prepares you to handle the success that is planned for you. Some doors in your life close off because life is full of tests, but the greatest tests are the test of discipline and the test of faith."

This insight prompted her to reflect on her situation. She questioned herself about what she should do next. Deciding against separation, she didn't want to follow in the footsteps of her mother-in-law and sister-in-law. Instead, she took charge of her life and decided to address the problem. She planned to have productive conversations with every family member.

Understanding the importance of living to fight another day, especially when dealing with people caught in toxic habits, she approached the situation with intelligence. Recognizing that toxic people often act irrationally, she decided not to engage emotionally and treated the challenge as a difficult task that required patience.

She embraced the belief that her dreams had no expiration date; she only needed to take a breath and try to fulfill them. Complaining about life seemed like a waste of time to her. Although it was natural to feel bad when treated poorly, she recognized that negative self-talk could create mental blockages and lead to a downward spiral.

She identified two major mental blocks that held her back: a feeling of helplessness and a fear of ignorance and abandonment. As she delved deeper into these fears and their origins, she realized that she needed to take responsibility for changing the course of her life. This awareness marked a significant step for her, acknowledging that the power to solve or overcome these challenges lay within her own hands.

After making this decision, she began to see herself as a warrior princess. She understood that the meaning in her life was something she could control; nothing around her had significance unless she chose to assign it meaning. With a strong belief in herself as a good woman with good intentions, she started to uncover and develop her hidden qualities. This newfound perspective empowered her to navigate through the challenges and embrace her role as the protagonist in her own life story.

HER TECHNIQUES TO BRING LIFE ON TRACK:

1. **Bringing Clarity in Mind:** She prioritizes clarity in her thoughts to effectively address family issues. By

understanding the root causes, she can work towards viable solutions.

2. **Life is About Creating, Not Finding:** Realizing that her satisfaction and happiness aren't dependent on others' opinions, she shifts her mindset from negative to positive. She acknowledges that behavioral patterns are generational and take time to change.

3. **Identifying the Source of Conflict:** She delves into understanding the source and depth of conflicts within the family, providing a foundation for resolving issues more effectively.

4. **Healthy Communication:** Choosing to share her feelings and patiently listen to others openly, she believes in the power of open communication for fostering a healthy family environment. Honest communication plays a crucial role in cultivating mutual respect.

5. **Compromising with Spouse:** Recognizing that some conflicts may not be easily resolved, she embraces compromise as a solution for the overall well-being of the family.

6. **Checking Emotions:** Even in the face of unresolved conflicts, she endeavors to remain calm and composed. Managing her emotions allows her to navigate through challenging situations, even if her spouse is not as composed.

7. **Be Willing to Forgive:** Recognizing the impact of holding grudges, she takes the initiative to forgive. Forgiveness becomes a powerful tool in resolving conflicts and moving forward.

8. **Routine for Well-Being:** She designs a routine for her life, incorporating elements like exercise and meditation. Each night, before sleep, she reflects on

whether she has given her best performance to live a fulfilling life.

9. **Choose Her Life Mission:** Identifying her life mission, she decides to provide emotional support and bring stability to her husband's life. Her commitment to creating a harmonious environment becomes a guiding principle.

10. **Become a Supportive Backbone:** Beyond her immediate family, she extends unwavering support to her mother-in-law and sister-in-law during tough times. This support not only helps them but also strengthens the bonds between them.

11. **Loving and Nurturing Attitude:** Embracing a loving and nurturing attitude, she becomes a catalyst for creating a peaceful atmosphere. Her love and care influence everyone around her, prompting positive changes in their attitudes.

12. **Promoting a Healthy Lifestyle:** Her unconditional love becomes a catalyst for mental well-being among all family members. Despite personal sacrifices, she finds the courage to break harmful patterns within her in-laws, understanding that change takes time and requires careful handling.

13. **Breaking Generational Impact:** Recognizing the generational impact of certain patterns, she makes a firm decision to stop this cycle from affecting future generations. She becomes a teacher and motivator for her mother-in-law, encouraging her to embrace change so that the family's future can be free from these detrimental influences.

14. **Teaching Adaptability Through Love:** With her love and support, she guides the family through changes, fostering adaptability for a healthier and more peaceful future. Love becomes the guiding force in helping

everyone navigate transitions and embrace positive transformations.

15. **Confidence in Herself:** Believing in herself empowers her to overcome challenges, take risks, and actively work towards the well-being of her family's future. This self-confidence becomes a driving force in her personal growth.
16. **Sense of Empowerment:** Taking control of her life makes a significant difference. Her proactive mindset, coupled with the initiative to encourage herself and work towards her goals, allows her to excel not only in her personal life but also in various aspects of her journey.
17. **Treating Her Husband with the Best Attitude:** She begins to appreciate her husband's concerns and dedication to the family. Adopting a positive attitude, she interacts with him as a happy and content woman, fostering a healthier relationship.
18. **Securing Her Legacy:** Her dream of creating a loving family comes to fruition. Recognizing that a loving family leaves a lasting legacy of success, prosperity, and happiness for generations to come, she takes pride in contributing to such a legacy.
19. **Exploring Her Husband's Emotions:** She invests time in understanding her husband's emotions and recognizing the sacrifices he makes for the family. This effort helps strengthen their bond and promotes mutual understanding in their relationship.

HER MISSION TO BE A RESPECTABLE WOMAN:

Being a respectable woman is a mission she embraces with dedication and grace. She understands that not everyone in life may value a good woman, but a man who does will appreciate her presence. Here are the qualities that define her mission:

1. **Balance and Peace-Loving Nature:** The first quality of a respectable woman is her ability to create balance in her relationship. She is a peace-loving person who respects herself and others in her life. Avoiding conflicts and family drama, she refuses to take unfair advantage of others.

2. **Well-Mannered and Gracious:** She carries herself with good manners and a positive attitude. Being the first to say sorry in a relationship, she expresses gratitude to everyone who contributes to her life. Her well-mannered and gracious demeanor extends to being a supportive spouse.

3. **Appreciation and Encouragement:** A respectable woman never takes her husband's efforts for granted. She appreciates and encourages him, avoiding the role of a complaining woman. She is aware that treating her husband with respect leads to being treated like a queen by society.

4. **Focus on Admirable Qualities:** Rather than dwelling on faults, she focuses on the admirable qualities of her husband. Every day, she prays for him, seeking transformation in their relationship. Being sympathetic and understanding, she fosters a supportive environment.

5. **Prayer for Strength and Unity:** In her daily prayers, she seeks peace of mind for her husband, asking for release from stress and clarity in decision-making. She prays for strength and power, emphasizing the importance of standing together through ups and downs.

6. **Give Respect and Gain Respect:** She follows the mantra of giving respect to gain respect and understand the reciprocal nature of relationships.
7. **Avoid Moody Attitudes:** Recognizing that being moody is not the right attitude for gaining respect, she chooses to be a happy woman to create a joyful home environment.
8. **Take Responsibility for Happiness:** Understanding that no one else is responsible for her happiness, she cultivates gratitude, composure, and responsibility to empower her own life.
9. **Own Your Feelings, Avoid Blame:** She takes responsibility for how she feels, refraining from blaming others or complaining. By owning her emotions, she maintains control over her responses to life's challenges.
10. **Stop Blaming, Take Responsibility:** Embracing the idea that life becomes easier when she stops blaming others and takes responsibility for her actions and choices.
11. **Power of Positive Emotion:** She harnesses the power of positive emotions, managing them productively to shape her thoughts, behaviors, and, ultimately, the results she experiences in her life.

Her mission as a respectable woman involves embodying qualities of balance, peace, gratitude, appreciation, and support.

HER HUSBAND'S CHANGED ATTITUDE - AN APOLOGY MESSAGE:

"My dear wife,

I never thought there would be days when the situation between us would get so challenging, and we might seem like falling apart. It's not that I doubt your love for me; there was a cloud in my thoughts. I was mad and cold towards you, not because I hated you, but because I was disappointed and didn't understand your perspective.

I never meant to hurt you, and I apologize for not understanding your intentions. Thank you for teaching me how to love. Sometimes, when I scream at you, it's not because I hate you; it's because my mind is out of control in anger.

I was tough on you because I know your potential. You handle family issues better than me. From now on, let's work as a team for a better future.

With love,

[His Name]"

MOST IMPORTANT HABITS TO ENHANCE YOUR RELATIONSHIP:

1. **Honest Communication:** The foundation of trust and transparency in a relationship is built on honest communication. Sharing the most sincere information with your spouse strengthens the bond between you.
2. **Teamwork:** Working together as a team is crucial for success in a relationship. Collaboration and mutual support create a strong foundation for navigating challenges and achieving shared goals.
3. **Joy, Peace, and Drama-Free Atmosphere:** Bringing joy and peace into your relationship while avoiding unnecessary drama fosters an environment of respect. A positive atmosphere contributes to the overall well-being of both partners.
4. **Respect for Others in the Family:** As a woman, showing respect for other women in your family is

essential. Avoid degrading others' values through negative gossip. Fostering a culture of respect contributes to a harmonious family dynamic.

These habits serve as pillars for a healthy and thriving relationship. Embracing honest communication, teamwork, a positive atmosphere, and respect for family members cultivate an environment where love and understanding can flourish.

Chapter 4:

TOGETHER LIVE A GREAT LIFE

Life is a precious gift that provides couples with the opportunity to weave a tapestry of shared experiences, creating memories that contribute to a fulfilling partnership. Through the highs and lows, couples have the chance to grow both individually and together, fostering personal development and a deeper connection.

Life becomes a gift for you both if you follow these values:

1. **Mutual Growth:** Embracing the chance for mutual growth, couples foster personal development and deeper connections. The ups and downs become opportunities for both individual and shared growth.
2. **Unconditional Support Through Challenges:** Life's challenges offer a platform for couples to provide unconditional support to each other. This support builds a strong foundation of trust and understanding, strengthening the bonds of the relationship.
3. **Companionship:** The journey of life becomes more enjoyable when shared with a life partner. Providing companionship during difficult times is a hallmark of being the best partner.
4. **Building and Nurturing a Family:** Couples take on the important duty of building and nurturing a family. Finding purpose and joy in watching their family grow becomes a fulfilling aspect of their shared journey.

5. **Learning from Differences:** Valuable lessons emerge from the differences between partners, fostering patience, empathy, and a deeper appreciation for each other's unique qualities.
6. **Emotional Dependency:** Couples experience and contribute to emotional dependency, creating a meaningful and fulfilling connection between them.
7. **Setting and Achieving Shared Goals:** Couples set and achieve shared goals, creating a sense of accomplishment that strengthens their bond.
8. **Celebrating Milestones:** Life offers moments to celebrate milestones, achievements, and special occasions, reinforcing the joy of shared success.
9. **Facing Challenges as a Team:** Facing life challenges as a team strengthens the bonds between a couple, instilling resilience and a sense of unity that enhances the overall fulfillment of their shared journey.

John Gray's book, *"Men Are from Mars, Women Are from Venus"*, sheds light on the unique communication styles and emotional needs of men and women. Recognizing and understanding these differences is key to fostering better communication and building stronger relationships.

MAJOR AREAS OF DIFFERENCE:

- **Sensitivity:**
  - Men tend to make decisions based on logic and problem-solving.
  - Women, on the other hand, often make decisions based on emotions and consideration of others' feelings.
    - Men may resist decisions influenced by emotions, preferring a more objective approach.

- **Communication:**
  - Men often prefer to solve problems on their own before sharing with others.
  - Women have a tendency to share their problems with their partners, hoping for collaborative solutions.
  - Men may resist listening to women's problems, leading to potential conflicts in communication styles.
- **Anger Expression:**
  - When men feel anger, they may express it through shouting or direct confrontation.
  - Women, on the other hand, may internalize anger, expressing it through tears, potentially leading to stress and depression.
- **Social Rejection:**
  - Women may prioritize others' needs and maintain a fulfilling attitude to avoid social rejection.
  - Women often enjoy social and cultural activities, while men may not always share the same enthusiasm for social gatherings.

FOUNDATION OF MARRIAGE:

The success of a marriage is deeply rooted in the foundation laid before and during the early years of matrimony. A strong foundation contributes to a healthy family structure, and three key principles play a pivotal role:

Equal or Similar Sharing Of Interests:

- Partners should share common interests or have a balanced approach to each other's hobbies and passions.

- This mutual sharing fosters a sense of togetherness and strengthens the bond between husband and wife.

Instant Sharing of Thoughts and Feelings:

- Open and immediate communication is crucial for a solid foundation.
- Partners should feel comfortable sharing their thoughts and feelings, creating an environment of transparency and understanding.

Harmony or Agreement of Each Other's Feelings:

- Harmony in emotional understanding is essential.
- Acknowledging and respecting each other's feelings, even in moments of disagreement, contributes to a harmonious relationship.

Family Structure and Responsibility:

- Proper administration of the family structure is vital for the well-being of individuals and society.
- The couple bears the responsibility of creating a conducive atmosphere for raising responsible individuals.
- Understanding the cultural significance of family and recognizing its role as the basic unit of society is crucial.

Financial Independence and Decision-Making:

- The couple should strive for financial independence to effectively manage responsibilities, especially those related to their children.
- They must make decisions together, taking ownership without passing blame to their parents.

Marriage as the Foundation of Family:
- The responsibility of a successful family lies with the new couple.
- While staying connected to their parents, they must independently decide and take responsibility for their children.
- The consequences of a faulty family foundation from previous generations can affect the present and future, emphasizing the importance of a strong start.

In essence, the success of a family is intricately tied to the choices, responsibilities, and foundation established by the couple in their marriage. A well-nurtured marriage forms the cornerstone of a flourishing family and, by extension, a thriving society.

Every family is guided by three fundamental principles, often considered the master plan of God. Understanding and properly applying these principles are key to the success of a family.

- **Leave:**
    - In the context of marriage, "leave" signifies the act of breaking dependency on one's parents to establish a new family with a spouse.
    - For a woman, leaving her parental home to join her husband's house is a symbolic transition.
    - The man takes on financial and social responsibilities independently, steering the course for the new family, and both partners assume responsibility for future generations.

- **Cleave:**
  - "Cleave" emphasizes the commitment of both husband and wife to remain faithful and dedicated to each other.
  - The primary intention of their marriage is to support and stand by each other through thick and thin.
  - This commitment forms the foundation of a strong marital bond, fostering mutual trust and unwavering support.

- **One-Flesh:**
  - "One-flesh" refers to the deep connection between two individuals who come together in marriage, forming an interdependent partnership.
  - It signifies a unity that goes beyond physical aspects, encompassing emotional, spiritual, and practical aspects of their lives.
  - The idea is to forge a profound connection that transcends individuality, creating a harmonious partnership.

If a family is experiencing difficulties, applying these three principles becomes crucial. A successful marriage and family depend on understanding and implementing these principles in daily life. By leaving dependency, cleaving to commitment, and embracing the concept of one-flesh unity, couples can navigate challenges and build a strong foundation for a thriving family.

Success is a divine gift bestowed upon those who take conscious and calculated steps in various aspects of life. The family, a divine creation, is intricately designed for success, with limitless potential if nurtured effectively.

The narrative begins with the first couple, Adam and Eve, created by God. This divine act signifies that marriage, an integral part of family life, is inherently linked to divinity. In the biblical account, God blessed Adam and Eve, instructing them to be fruitful and replenish the earth. This blessing establishes a foundational understanding that God intended the human family to thrive through divine guidance.

Success in family life encompasses four essential areas: health, money, career, and relationships. These pillars, when harmoniously aligned, contribute to an overall sense of fulfillment and prosperity.

The divine blueprint of the family, created by God, is not rooted in pressure, grief, or lack of prosperity. Instead, it is a framework designed to foster pleasure, happiness, and success through the infusion of divine energy. The primary role in this divine design is bestowed upon man, who plays a central role in steering the family towards success.

In recognizing this divine connection, individuals can approach family life with a sense of purpose and responsibility. By aligning with the principles set forth by the Creator, one can unlock the potential for success in health, wealth, career, and relationships within the family unit.

The divine intention is clear: families are meant to flourish, and success is an inherent part of this divine plan. Through conscious efforts, adherence to divine principles, and recognizing the role of each family member, the journey of family life unfolds as a path toward divine success.

DUTIES OF MEN IN FAMILY LIFE: BALANCING RESPONSIBILITIES AND EXPECTATIONS

As the head of the family, men bear a significant responsibility for the welfare of their family, extending beyond just their spouse and children to encompass parents, siblings, and relatives. Despite potential challenges and pressures, fulfilling these duties is crucial for maintaining a harmonious family dynamic:

1. Comprehensive Responsibility:
- A man's family includes not only his immediate family but also his parents, siblings, and relatives.
- Despite potential challenges or lack of reciprocation, fulfilling his duty towards all family members is paramount.

2. Balancing Priorities:
- Men often find themselves torn between responsibilities towards their parents and their new family with a spouse.
- Balancing these priorities requires effective communication and understanding with both sets of family members.

3. Effective Communication:
- Men may struggle to express their feelings and concerns to both parents and spouses, leading to misunderstandings.
- Prioritizing open and effective communication is crucial for maintaining healthy relationships.

4. Financial Responsibility:
- The primary breadwinner faces challenges in balancing financial responsibility for both parents and spouse.
- Striking a balance and ensuring financial stability is crucial for the well-being of the entire family.

5. Adjusting to Changes:

- Adjusting to the changes that come with marriage, such as juggling roles as a son, husband, and father, can create stress.
- Adapting to new responsibilities requires resilience and a willingness to navigate evolving family dynamics.

GOOD QUALITIES EXPECTED:

- **Sharing Every Emotion:** A perfect man is open about his emotions and shares them with his spouse.
- **Maintaining Self-Control:** In times of conflict, a man with self-control can navigate issues calmly and maturely.
- **Good Reputation in Community:** A positive reputation in the community reflects positively on the family.
- **Good Communication Skills:** Effective communication is key to understanding and resolving issues.
- **Mastering Problem Handling:** A man adept at handling problems contributes to a stable family environment.
- **Protective Nature:** A sense of protectiveness towards his spouse fosters a secure and supportive atmosphere.
- **Giving Credit and Appreciation:** Acknowledging and appreciating the efforts of his spouse contributes to a positive relationship.
- **Showing Maturity:** Maturity in handling relationship dynamics is essential for a successful and fulfilling family life.

DUTIES OF WOMEN IN FAMILY LIFE: NURTURING, PRAYER, AND SUPPORT

Women play a pivotal role in maintaining the well-being of the family, and their duties encompass various aspects, from prayer to fostering a supportive and encouraging atmosphere. Here are some key responsibilities and qualities expected of women in family life:

1. Sobriety and Love for Family:
- Women are expected to maintain a calm and sober attitude, fostering an atmosphere of love within the family.

2. Prioritizing Responsibilities:
- The primary duties of women are directed towards God, followed by elders, husbands, and then children.
- Prioritizing responsibilities ensures a balanced and harmonious family life.

3. Prayer for Well-Being:
- A woman's primary duty is to pray for the well-being of her family.
- Her prayers are seen as a protective shield for the home and its inhabitants.

4. Protector of Dignity:
- Women are entrusted with the duty to protect the dignity of their husbands.
- Acknowledging and appreciating the efforts of the husband is essential, and criticism should be avoided.

5. Encouragement and Admiration:
- Rather than being a complaining woman, a wife is encouraged to appreciate and encourage her husband.
- Compliments and admiration can provide the husband with the energy and motivation to face life's challenges.

QUALITIES EXPECTED OF WOMEN:

- **Honest and Trustworthy:** Women are expected to uphold honesty and trustworthiness in all aspects of family life.
- **Intelligent and Curious:** An intelligent and curious nature contributes to a dynamic and engaging family environment.
- **Self-Confident and Graceful:** Confidence and gracefulness enhance a woman's ability to navigate various situations in family life.
- **Compassionate and Forgiving:** Compassion and a forgiving nature foster understanding and harmony within the family.
- **Kind and Thoughtful:** Kindness and thoughtfulness create a nurturing atmosphere for family members.
- **Down to Earth:** Being down to earth helps maintain humility and understanding in family relationships.
- **Open to Learning:** A willingness to learn ensures adaptability and growth within the family unit.
- **Less Complaining Attitude:** Minimizing complaints and focusing on solutions contributes to a positive family environment.

PARENTAL DUTIES: NURTURING COMMUNICATION AND BREAKING THE CYCLE

Parental duties extend beyond providing physical care to nurturing a positive and communicative atmosphere within the family. Here are essential aspects of parental responsibilities, focusing on effective communication and breaking the cycle of negativity:

- **Setting a Positive Example:**
    - Parents play a crucial role as role models for their children.
    - The children often mirror behaviors and attitudes displayed by parents.

- **Avoiding Unhealthy Conflicts:**
    - Constant quarreling and fighting between parents can negatively impact children.
    - Strive to create a harmonious environment, avoiding conflicts that may affect the well-being of the family.

- **Breaking the Cycle of Unhappiness:**
    - Acknowledge the potential impact of parental behaviors on the future lives of children.
    - Make a conscious effort to break the cycle of unhappiness by fostering a positive and supportive family atmosphere.

- **Releasing Emotions and Forgiveness:**
    - Emphasize the importance of releasing negative emotions like offense, misunderstanding, and hurt.

- Unforgiveness is compared to cancer, eating away at peace and family values. Encourage forgiveness to heal emotional wounds.

- **Effective Communication:**
  - Facilitate open and effective communication between parents.
  - Encourage both partners to share their thoughts and feelings freely, creating a two-sided communication process.

- **Learning from Communication Breakdowns:**
  - Recognize that faulty communication is a common contributor to marital breakdowns.
  - Instead of allowing communication breakdowns to lead to arguments, adopt healthier communication methods to foster understanding.

- **Avoiding Assumptions:**
  - Assumptions can limit communication and understanding in relationships.
  - Encourage open dialogue to prevent misunderstandings and assumptions from becoming barriers.

- **Building Emotional Connection:**
  - Good communication is essential for understanding each other's needs and feelings.
  - Foster emotional connections by communicating effectively, and building a healthier and more resilient relationship.

- **Creating a Two-Way Communication Channel:**
  - Establish a communication channel where both partners can share their thoughts and feelings freely.
  - Encourage active listening to create a supportive and empathetic environment.

- **Encouraging Healthy Communication Patterns:**
  - Teach children about healthy communication patterns.
  - Equip them with the skills to express themselves effectively and understand the importance of resolving conflicts positively.

STEPS FOR BETTER UNDERSTANDING BETWEEN PARENTS AND CHILDREN:

Building a strong and understanding relationship between parents and children involves intentional efforts and effective communication. Here are crucial steps to foster understanding:

Active Listening:

- Pay close attention to what your spouse or child is saying.
- Practice active listening to ensure a deeper understanding of their thoughts and feelings.

Open Communication:

- Encourage honest and clear expression of thoughts and emotions.
- Create an environment where everyone feels comfortable sharing their feelings openly.

Empathy:

- Seek to understand the feelings of your spouse or child.
- Foster empathy to create a supportive and understanding family atmosphere.

Choose the Right Time:

- Select appropriate times for communication, free from distractions.
- Avoid initiating important discussions during times of stress or potential arguments.

Patience:

- Cultivate patience, especially during times of disagreement or argument.
- Stay calm and composed to navigate through challenging situations.

Problem Solving Together:

- Approach challenges as a team rather than placing blame.
- Work collaboratively to find solutions and address issues constructively.

Appreciation:

- Express gratitude and appreciation regularly.
- Acknowledge each other's efforts and contributions to the family.

Quality Time:

- Spend quality time together as a family.

- Engage in activities that strengthen the bond and create lasting connections.

Respect Boundaries:

- Understand and respect the boundaries of each family member.
- Recognize the importance of personal space and individual needs.

Understanding the impact of your personality on your parenting and relationship dynamics is a crucial aspect of creating a harmonious family environment. Children are highly perceptive and often mimic the behaviors and interactions they witness with their parents. Therefore, it becomes essential for parents to reflect on their personalities and how they influence the family atmosphere.

Start by looking into your family history and examining the traits inherited from your parents and grandparents. Identify both the strengths and weaknesses in their personalities, understanding how these factors contributed to their successes or challenges in life. By gaining clarity on the family's past, you can determine what aspects to embrace and what to improve upon.

Introspection is a powerful tool in personal development. Reflect on your own personality — the characteristics you are proud of and those you wish to rectify. Consider how your behaviors and attitudes contribute to the overall dynamics of your family. This self-awareness is the first step towards positive change.

Once you've gained clarity about your personality, extend the same understanding to your spouse. Open and honest communication about your self-reflections can deepen the connection between you and your partner. Share your aspirations for personal growth and encourage your spouse to do the same. This process of mutual introspection can create a supportive environment where both partners actively contribute to each other's development.

The benefits of being aware of your own personality and that of your spouse are manifold. It fosters a sense of togetherness and closeness as you work collaboratively towards creating a family atmosphere that aligns with your shared values and aspirations. The willingness to grow and evolve as individuals not only strengthens the bond between partners but also sets a positive example for children, who learn valuable life skills from observing their parents navigate challenges with self-awareness and open communication.

A devoted wife stands by her husband during tough times because she recognizes the goodness in him. Even when he's going through difficulties, she stays by his side because she sees unique qualities in him. She understands that facing challenges together is not in vain and believes that they will harvest success together. It's important for a man to realize that a woman knows where to invest her emotions. She chooses to invest in someone she believes will yield worthwhile results.

If your wife has faith in you, why give up on yourself? Show her that her belief in you is well-placed. A confident man catches her attention – she observes how he handles problems with assurance, his mannerisms, how he treats others, his ambition, and even his sense of style. All these aspects stimulate her admiration for him.

On the flip side, when a man is married, navigating through financial difficulties can bring about emotional pain. The strain of financial challenges may lead to stress and disagreements within the couple. Differences in values or goals can create a sense of disconnection, contributing to emotional distress. Even when both partners are earning, the stress of managing shared finances might result in conflicts, especially if there are varying spending habits or priorities.

Therefore, couples need to have open communication about money matters.

Men facing financial challenges within marriage may also grapple with additional responsibilities, such as new living arrangements and obligations towards parents and in-laws.

Achieving a balance between these responsibilities can be challenging. Often, men find themselves torn and strained, trying to manage these priorities. Men tend to conceal their pain, particularly during financial breakdowns, pretending that everything is fine. Hence, establishing open communication between couples becomes crucial in addressing these challenges and maintaining a healthy relationship.

Once, a young lady visited her mother's house after getting married, expressing her concern that her husband wasn't interested in buying the things she desired. The mother, in response, questioned how many things she had purchased for her husband and whether he complained about it. The young lady fell silent and replied, "But he is my husband. It's his duty to buy for me." The mother wisely advised, "Don't assess his love for you based on the things he buys. Love goes beyond material possessions."

In the early stages of marriage, there's often financial pressure on a man, and it's important for a wife to understand her husband's struggles. One day, upon returning home, the lady overheard her husband alone, pouring his heart out to God. He was crying, seeking help to earn more to meet the needs of his family, including responsibilities like his sister's marriage, his parents' health issues, and his wife's needs. Touched by this revelation, the lady broke down, realizing the depth of her husband's pain, even though he never complained.

Some wives may view their husbands as superheroes, but it's crucial to accept that they might be facing challenges and may not have the capacity to afford all the material things desired. The reality is when a woman starts earning, she might feel a sense of independence, while a man, upon earning, often takes on the responsibility of the entire family. Although rich men may marry women from less affluent backgrounds, it's noted that rich women may be hesitant to consider a less affluent man.

Therefore, it's true that the financial responsibility of the family traditionally falls on the husband, but modern couples are increasingly sharing these responsibilities. Many family issues often stem from financial problems, emphasizing the importance of open communication and mutual understanding in navigating these challenges together.

In an exceptional relationship, the two of you possess the potential to build a truly wonderful world for yourselves and your children. It's important to recognize that the magnitude of your responsibilities surpasses the understanding of friends, extended family, and relatives. In this story, you are both the authors and the heroes, standing tall to face everyday challenges together.

Together, as a husband and wife, you form a powerful mastermind capable of creating a life that is both prosperous and fulfilling. By unlocking the inherent power and strength within you, working together with a mindset of prosperity and wealth, you'll not only find greater happiness but also craft an ideal family image. Embrace the journey, face each day united, and watch as your collective efforts shape a world uniquely yours.

Strength in a family doesn't mean that both husband and wife are equally strong in every aspect of life. The rule is simple: you either win together or lose together. Therefore, face every challenge hand in hand, working together to find solutions to your problems. As parents, both of you serve as models for your children, setting examples for the kind of relationship that will inspire your son to become a good husband and your daughter to grow up into a good wife.

Your dream life is not just an imagination; it is a reality waiting to be created. Together, create a life filled with authenticity, nurturing a relationship that is strong and supportive. Take the time to appreciate the things in your life, and in doing so, you'll be weaving a tapestry of strength, love, and resilience that forms the foundation of a truly strong family.

Marriage takes couples through various emotional stages, and recognizing these phases is key to managing emotions effectively. In the initial stage, the "New Beginning," marriages often start with hope, joy, and excitement. Both partners approach it with optimism, gratitude, love, and trust.

The second stage involves difficulties, typically arising from how a couple responds to challenging situations. During this time, emotions like hurt, anger, disappointment, and loneliness may intensify. Attitudes turn negative, and frustration sets in. Communication breaks down, leading to arguments, and if not addressed, this stage can result in divorce or separation.

The third stage is the outcome of how well the couple navigated the challenges of the second stage. If they handle it with patience and nurture the relationship through sacrifice, the third stage can bring about a peaceful and satisfied life. It underscores the importance of weathering difficulties together to enjoy the rewards of a resilient and enduring marriage.

Chapter 5:

STOP MESSING WITH FUTURE GENERATIONS

Family plays a crucial role in offering ongoing support through life's ups and downs. Whether we're rejoicing in achievements or facing setbacks, our family is there to share the journey. Yet, it's only natural that disagreements and misunderstandings can arise.

Everyday conflicts among family members are common, but sometimes these issues linger, causing persistent tension over the years. Extended conflicts and instances of violence can have lasting effects on the mental and physical well-being of children within the family.

Dysfunctional families often form when persistent conflicts, alcohol addiction, single parenting, unemployment, and mental illness create ongoing tension. In such families, members tend to adopt the same perspectives and behavior patterns, living by a set of norms that may not be healthy. When someone within the family tries to break these established patterns, it's seen as going against the "rules."

Children raised in such environments often experience unhappiness and loneliness. As they grow older and start families of their own, they may unintentionally replicate the dysfunctional patterns, perpetuating a cycle of disturbance.

No family is without imperfections; every family encounters stress and pain from time to time. In a healthy family, issues are resolved with love, respect, trust, and support.

It's normal for spouses to have disagreements, but certain behaviors can turn a family dysfunctional, especially when:

1. **Maintaining Secrets:** Keeping secrets instead of open communication can create distance and mistrust within the family.
2. **Avoiding Communication:** Refusing to talk about problems and avoiding communication hinders the resolution of issues.
3. **Addictions or Unhealthy Habits:** If one of the partners engages in harmful activities like illicit affairs, alcoholism, excessive video gaming, being domineering, or displaying abusive behavior, it can severely impact the family.
4. **Unrealistic Expectations from Children:** Expecting children to shoulder responsibilities beyond their age can lead to stress and hinder their normal development.

Building a healthy family system involves mutual nurturing and support between husband and wife. Together, they should care for and nurture their children, fostering a sense of emotional well-being within the family. It's common for couples to face challenges related to health, wealth, and career, but it's important not to place blame on oneself or one's spouse.

The parents of the couple also play a significant role in the family dynamic. While they possess valuable experience in married life, sometimes they may hesitate to guide or positively support the younger couple.

After marriage, a woman enters her husband's house to establish a new family. It's unfair to blame a daughter-in-law for issues in the family. She is a new member who lacks experience regarding the habits, attitudes, and behaviors of her husband's family. Understanding each other's nature and thoughts takes time.

Instead of blaming your wife for family problems or strained relations with your parents, it's essential to realize that you spent 20 to 30 years understanding your parents before marriage. You are better aware of their thoughts, attitudes, and behaviors. It's crucial not to shift the entire responsibility onto your wife. When you care for your parents, your wife will learn from you.

If you and your parents start blaming her, be prepared for a potential breakdown in trust. This blaming dynamic can lead to detachment in the family bond, laying the foundation for dysfunction. Once the blaming game starts, it often continues, leaving behind an unhealthy family legacy for your children.

When a husband actively takes care of his wife's physical, emotional, and spiritual well-being, he brings out the best version of her behavior. In such a supportive environment, she is more likely to contribute wholeheartedly to the family's growth, taking care of both the husband's parents and children. Without the fear of survival, she can flourish and showcase her best qualities.

It's crucial to recognize that a woman's behavior often reflects how she has been treated. If a husband and his parents have wronged her emotionally, she may mirror the impact of those actions. If you find yourself unhappy with her current behavior, it's essential to reflect on how you treated her in the past.

After marriage, some parents continue to treat their son as if he's still a boy. Parents need to recognize that their son has become a partner to a woman and that woman seeks a responsible and capable life partner. A wife respects a man who can make decisions and handle responsibilities. If a husband fails in these aspects, his wife may feel insecure about their future together.

In this emotional struggle, wives may find their expectations and suggestions consistently rejected in the presence of the husband's parents. The parents, driven by the fear of losing their son, often turn a blind eye to support him and stand against their daughter-in-law. What was once disliked about the son's behavior before marriage may become acceptable, especially if he uses those behaviors to punish his wife. To avoid creating an insecure environment for daughters-in-law, every woman needs to raise her son in a way that prepares him for a partnership.

In contemporary times, the role of the mother-in-law can sometimes contribute to challenges within a family. A man once expressed his frustration, sharing that he harbored feelings of dislike for his in-laws because they didn't give enough space in his relationship with his wife. The constant presence of the wife's parents, coupled with their opinions and expectations, led to ongoing issues.

Additionally, the mother-in-law underestimated the husband's financial situation, causing further strain.

It is crucial for parents to guide their children to navigate shared happiness and to nurture their physical, emotional, social, and material well-being.

A mother dedicates herself to raising her son, investing her time and energy without always considering her own health. Similarly, when a wife chooses to leave her home to build a life with her husband, she steps out of her comfort zone, makes compromises, and dedicates her youth to nurturing their relationship.

In the complex dynamics between a man, his mother, and his wife, misunderstandings can lead to a cold war that disrupts the peace in his married life. The mother may perceive the wife as wanting to separate them, while the wife may feel the mother is trying to control their married life. In this tug-of-war, family members may play tricks to defend or criticize the wife, leaving the man confused and leading to blame directed at his spouse.

The consequences of this situation can result in a loss of appreciation from family and a lack of respect from the wife. Both husband and wife need to be aware of their actions and the potential outcomes. Taking responsibility for their roles in the relationship is crucial for building a positive future.

As the situation escalates, men may experience depression and stress, expressing their feelings through anger towards their wives. This emotional turmoil arises from unrealistic expectations placed on the wife before marriage, expecting her to be a problem-solving angel and a magician capable of bringing all-round development and happiness to his life and family.

Emotional wounds and trauma aren't just sources of pain but significant obstacles to growth. Some individuals view them as sources of strength and insight, choosing a challenging path to break patterns. Recognition is key — identifying which patterns are gifts from ancestors and which hinder the creation of a successful present and future generation.

When someone attempts to create a new pattern or challenge existing norms, they are often met with resistance from others. If you want to change a situation, it's essential to start by changing yourself. Emotions such as love, abandonment, shame, and anxiety can influence your interactions with family members.

To navigate these emotional complexities, it's important to manage your thoughts effectively. Being overly cautious about the potential for criticism, disapproval, or cold behavior from your spouse or other family members can lead to confusion. This heightened sensitivity may prompt you to question your thoughts and perceptions, creating a sense of uncertainty within yourself.

Experiencing a decline in confidence and relying heavily on the attitudes of your spouse and other family members can significantly impact your emotional well-being. Expecting better behavior and support from them may lead to heightened stress, creating a cycle of worry and confusion.

The fear of an unpredictable or moody reaction from your spouse can make you hyper-aware of your actions and words as you strive to avoid further problems. This constant state of worry and uncertainty becomes particularly challenging for a woman when her husband and his parents resort to silent treatment and non-cooperation. Despite her sacrifices, she may feel powerless and helpless, entering an uncomfortable stage of life.

In large families with diverse personalities and behavioral patterns, maintaining a peaceful environment can be challenging. Understanding each person's personality and needs becomes crucial. Parents, especially mothers, often navigate the complexities of parenting and managing various relationships amidst the hustle. Recognizing the individuality of each family member and finding a balance becomes essential for fostering harmony in such dynamic family settings.

Here are some techniques for women to support themselves:

1. **Self-Care Approach:** Treat yourself with the same care and love that you would extend to someone you want to help. Prioritize your physical and mental health to become the best version of yourself.
2. **Establish Clear Boundaries:** Set clear boundaries for the behavior of your spouse and children, emphasizing the importance of respectful treatment. It's essential to communicate and uphold these boundaries consistently.
3. **Personal Boundaries:** Establish personal boundaries for yourself, taking responsibility for solving your own problems. Avoid excessive irritation towards your husband, and be truthful in your communication to build trust in your relationship.
4. **Clear Communication:** Be clear and open in your communication. Avoid assumptions and express your thoughts and feelings openly. Clarity fosters understanding and helps in resolving issues more effectively.
5. **Open-Minded Growth:** Cultivate an open-minded attitude that contributes to personal growth. Embrace new perspectives and experiences that can enhance your overall well-being.
6. **Avoid Excessive Compromise:** While compromise is essential in any relationship, avoid compromising to the extent that it negatively impacts your own well-being. Strike a balance that ensures your happiness and fulfillment.
7. **Realistic Expectations:** Avoid setting unrealistic expectations for your husband, understanding that too much romance or constant availability may not be

sustainable. Realistic expectations contribute to a healthier and more balanced relationship.

Here are some techniques for creating a peaceful family environment:

1. **Avoid Hurting Your Wife:** Refrain from hurting your wife, as actions often reciprocate. Treat her with kindness and respect to nurture a positive relationship.
2. **Manage Anger and Frustration:** Avoid displaying anger and frustration towards your wife, especially when she is not responsible for the situation. Practice communication and understanding instead of venting frustrations.
3. **Perfection is Unattainable:** Acknowledge that a perfect partner doesn't exist. Strive to be a perfect man with a realistic vision of life, embracing imperfections in the relationship.
4. **Take Responsibility:** Take responsibility for your decisions and actions. Shape your own life without placing blame on your wife, fostering a sense of empowerment and accountability.
5. **Embrace Failure and Make Your Own Luck:** Learn to embrace failure as part of the journey and take proactive steps to create your own luck. Avoid bringing frustration home, as it can negatively impact your wife and children.
6. **Commit to Goals:** If you have goals, commit to them wholeheartedly. Don't expect your wife to bring prosperity if you're not dedicated to your own aspirations. Address any attitude problems and focus on finding solutions.

ROLE OF MOTHERS IN A COUPLE'S LIFE:

The role of the mother in the lives of both the husband and wife is pivotal, influencing how they relate to and respect each other. A woman learns from her mother how to love and respect a man and, in turn, how to receive respect from him. The foundation of this understanding is often laid during their formative years, observing the interactions between their parents.

For a man, his relationship with his mother shapes his perception of how to treat women. If he learns to respect his mother, he is likely to extend the same courtesy to his wife. The manner in which he communicates and interacts with his mother serves as a blueprint for his interactions with his spouse.

Similarly, a woman's attitude toward her father plays a crucial role in her relationships. If she has a positive and respectful attitude toward her father, she is more likely to carry those qualities into her marriage. Adoration for her father may translate into a similar admiration and respect for her husband.

The cycle of wounded relationships can have a lasting impact, passing down unhealthy attitudes from one generation to the next. A woman who has experienced emotional wounds in her own relationships may inadvertently pass on these attitudes to her children. Similarly, an abusive father may unknowingly pass on this damaging legacy to his son.

The modeled behavior of parents becomes a powerful influence on the future legacy of the family. A mistreated daughter-in-law, if not healed from past trauma, may carry those unresolved emotions into her role as a mother-in-law. Compromises made in her own married life might lead her to see her son as a substitute for her husband and his daughter-in-law in her place.

This lack of awareness about the emotional impact of her actions can lead her to play the "mother card" with the couple, forgetting the toll interference took on her own life. To break this cycle, individuals need to address and heal from past wounds. Both parents of the newlyweds should understand the importance of allowing the couple to explore and solve their own issues without unnecessary interference.

Unhealthy family behavior extends beyond abuse and negligence; it includes engaging in damaging gossip and undermining each other before emotional healing has occurred.

STORY OF A JOINT FAMILY:

Shelly entered a joint family at the age of 27, transitioning from her calm nuclear family of four members to a bustling environment with around ten members. On her first day, she encountered a different culture and tradition, notably the Indian custom where newlyweds touch the feet of elders for blessings. This was a stark contrast to her radical upbringing.

Feeling frustrated, Shelly found the tradition challenging, while her husband, accustomed to the practice, performed it effortlessly. In a teasing manner, he welcomed her to the "grand family," acknowledging the significant shift she was experiencing in her new life.

Shelly, a working professional, initially worried about how to adjust to the dynamics of a big extended family in the joint family system, where maximum adjustment is required. After a few months, she began to realize that all the family members were loving and caring. Despite the warmth, Shelly found herself still struggling to adjust to the constant hustle of the household.

The house was always full of people, with a continuous flow of guests making it noisy. Socialization and entertainment were integral parts of the household routine, with frequent parties, outings, and holiday plans. Shelly navigated the balance between her professional life and the vibrant, socially active environment of her joint family.

After the first year of marriage, Shelly began feeling the interference of others in her life. Everyone had opinions on when she should have a child and suggestions about her job, which became frustrating. Interestingly, Shelly noticed that during disagreements with her husband, her mother-in-law consistently took her side, contrary to the common perception of mothers-in-law favoring their sons.

Shelly's husband's parents played a positive role, teaching him how to maintain balance in married life. This dynamic contributed to a happy relationship between Shelly, her husband, and his mother. Despite external pressures, the family harmony prevailed, creating a supportive environment.

Shelly realized that a happy family is not something given; it is something you have to create. Her parents-in-law used to welcome her parents with respect and treat them in the best possible way, setting a positive example. The family members maintained good communication with each other, fostering an atmosphere of love, respect, adjustment, and forgiveness.

Living in a joint family after marriage proved to be healthier for Shelly due to the family's adaptability and willingness to forgive. These values became even more significant when Shelly became a mother, and she strived to pass on the same ethos of love, respect, and understanding to the next generation.

As Shelly became a mother, she found tremendous support from her extended family. Even when she was at work, her children never felt neglected due to the robust support system provided by family members. This experience made Shelly appreciate her family even more, considering herself fortunate to have such a strong support network.

Living in a joint family had its benefits — loneliness was never a factor. The children grew up surrounded by love, easily learning the art of socialization. They became adept at adjusting to new environments and embracing challenges with resilience, thanks to the nurturing environment provided by the joint family structure.

When Shelly's husband expressed concern about their son's excessive cellphone use, Shelly pointed out that he, too, used a laptop and mobile until late at night. Her father-in-law overheard the conversation and decided to take action against this shared addiction.

Together, the family devised a plan: they declared one day a week as a "no mobile day." On this day, everyone put away their phones, laptops, and televisions. Instead, they engaged in conversations, played together, and took the opportunity to teach the children various skills, such as cooking and organization. This intentional break from technology became a weekly tradition, contributing to the healing of the addiction and fostering meaningful family connections.

The greatest gift a family can give to their children is a life that is healed. Parenting challenges often stem from insecurities rooted in the desire to protect our children from the trauma or harm we experienced. Unconsciously, we may pass down negative thoughts and habits to our children.

Thus, healing becomes essential for cultivating a healthy family life.

Finding the need for healing involves introspection and asking yourself some important questions:

1. **Family Patterns:** Are there any family patterns that you carry but dislike? Do these patterns negatively affect your relationships and pose a threat to your future?
2. **Powerlessness and Helplessness:** Have you ever felt powerless and helpless in managing your behavior or handling certain situations?
3. **Sugarcoating Relationships:** Are you sugarcoating aspects of your relationship to hide the truth due to fear of damaging your family's reputation?
4. **Skills Gap:** Are you lacking in money management and communication skills, and is it impacting your life?
5. **Forgiveness and Forgetfulness:** Do you struggle with forgetting and forgiving? Are unresolved issues affecting your well-being?
6. **Conflict Resolution:** How do you prefer to handle conflicts within your family? Is there room for improvement in this area?
7. **Family Activities:** What kinds of family activities do you enjoy? How do these activities contribute to the overall family dynamic?
8. **Approach to Traditions and Rituals:** How do you approach family traditions and rituals? Are they a source of joy or stress?
9. **Expression of Appreciation and Forgiveness:** How do you express appreciation and forgiveness within your family?

10. **Managing Relationships:** As a man, do you find it challenging to balance your relationship with your mother and wife? Do you experience depression in managing these relationships?
11. **Communication with Parents:** Do you feel nervous about discussing family issues with your parents?
12. **Interference and Emotional Imbalance:** Do you sense interference from others in your life, and is your emotional imbalance impacting your relationships?

If you find that any of these questions resonate with your experiences, it may indicate a need for personal healing. Acknowledging and addressing these areas can contribute to a healthier and more fulfilling life.

Chapter 6:

HEALING

To lead a truly fulfilling life, consider being the boss of your own thoughts, habits, beliefs, and actions — it's like steering your own ship.

There are four zones you must steer away from your life to build a successful and happy family. Every tough moment we face is just a chapter in our life story, helping us grow.

Our purpose in this life is to be part of a love revolution, where we discover how to love ourselves and break free from feeling like a victim of our past.

Building a family becomes meaningful when we see it as a small but purposeful piece in the vast puzzle of the universe and humanity.

As grown-ups, when we actively work on improving ourselves and let go of negative influences, we release a positive energy that can reshape our lives. Adjacently, this grooms us to work for the well-being of our community as a whole.

To cleanse our inner self and foster growth, taking intentional actions in these four zones can make a significant difference:

Comfort Zone:

- Step out of your comfort zone by fostering open communication. Share fears and goals with each other.
- Actively compromise to ensure each other's happiness, facing challenges as a united front.

Blame Zone:

- Avoid blaming your spouse or parents; it doesn't contribute to personal growth. Take joint responsibility for both failures and successes.
- Develop the skills of active listening and empathy, seeking solutions together. Cultivate a positive atmosphere through appreciation and forgiveness.

Anger Zone:

- Minimize unnecessary drama in life and refrain from emotional manipulation. Expressing anger or resorting to silent treatment may boost your ego temporarily but can lead to detachment.
- Create an environment of detachment to avoid relying solely on emotional support from your partner.

Hurt Zone:

- Establish boundaries for self-respect in your relationship; don't allow yourself to be treated as a doormat.
- Prioritize your mental and physical well-being; don't sacrifice without receiving anything in return.
- Explore different habits that ensure your safety and happiness, avoiding actions that can hurt yourself or allow others to harm you.

Throughout their lives, many couples find themselves caught up in blame rather than understanding each other. Society and family often contribute to this divide, evaluating individuals based on their attitudes and behaviors.

In our culture, a man earns respect for his financial stability, integrity, and problem-solving skills, with judgment based on how he handles challenges and his societal responsibilities.

Conversely, a woman is appreciated for her humility, kindness, and intellectual prowess, with her beauty shining even brighter when coupled with intelligence.

However, both genders need to realize that a woman's dedication to society shouldn't overshadow her responsibilities toward her family.

The true essence of a fulfilling life lies in understanding and supporting each other, transcending societal expectations, and fostering a partnership where both individuals can thrive personally and contribute to society.

Life indeed presents its fair share of expectations, struggles, and adversities, leaving limited time for enjoying moments of happiness and success. This is a universal rule. However, working together can make life easier for both partners. The challenge often lies in the role of expectations, which can contribute to differences between them.

Women often dream of a highly compatible man who understands and shares their aspirations for personal and collective growth.

The ideal man, in this context, is someone with whom they can forge a deep emotional connection. They seek a partner who provides support, empathy, and understanding —

someone capable of offering a sense of security both emotionally and physically.

The dream is of a person who can provide unconditional love, acceptance, and companionship, creating a harmonious and fulfilling life together.

For a man, the dream often involves finding a woman who brings joy and balance into his life.

This ideal partner is someone who can foster strong connections among family members, making relationships not just functional but genuinely enjoyable. The man envisions a companion with a compassionate and understanding nature, someone who shares similar habits and interests.

The ideal woman, in his eyes, possesses the quality of bringing balance to their life — creating a harmonious and fulfilling partnership where both individuals can thrive and find happiness together.

Mutual understanding and trust are the cornerstones of the dream relationship in both cases.

NAVIGATE YOUR LIFE WITH THE PURPOSE OF HEALING:

Begin the healing process by establishing clear boundaries between both of you, grounded in your likes and dislikes. Contrary to creating distance, boundaries serve to bring you closer, fostering mutual respect and understanding.

This foundation sets the stage for personal and family growth. Concentrate on nurturing these qualities to enhance your journey:

Courage:

- Courage is a key factor in balancing one's life, enabling the ability to face challenges and make difficult decisions.
- It empowers individuals to step outside their comfort zones and pursue personal goals, contributing to personal growth.
- By modeling courage, you can teach your children how to confront fear and adversity, fostering a balanced and fulfilling life.

Resilience:

- Resilience provides the strength to bounce back from adversity and adapt to changing circumstances.
- Individuals with resilience tend to handle stress more effectively and maintain a positive outlook, contributing to life's balance.
- Developing resilience supports emotional well-being and helps maintain stability in the face of life's challenges.

Empathy:

- Empathy enhances relationships and facilitates more effective navigation of conflicts.
- By empathizing, individuals develop a deeper awareness of emotions, leading to better emotional regulation and stress management.
- This emotional intelligence contributes to a more harmonious and fulfilling life, both personally and within the family. Prioritizing understanding and connecting with your partner's emotions is crucial.

Integrity:

- Integrity forms the bedrock for trust in relationships and cultivates a deep sense of self-respect.
- It serves as a guiding principle for ethical decision-making, contributing to a balanced life.
- Upholding integrity enables a couple to navigate life with honesty and authenticity, fostering a more harmonious and balanced existence.

Passion:

- Pursuing activities with passion enhances overall well-being and nurtures a positive mindset.
- Passion acts as a motivating force, aiding in managing challenges in various aspects of life.
- It contributes to a harmonious equilibrium by allowing the allocation of time and energy to both responsibilities and activities that bring joy, fostering mental and emotional balance.

Adaptability:

- In families, both men and women play diverse roles, requiring flexibility and balance.
- Effective time management and maintaining health equilibrium are essential to meet personal, professional, and family needs.
- Embracing adaptability involves adjusting priorities based on changing circumstances and learning from experiences to break recurring patterns, fostering a more balanced and resilient family life.

Mindfulness:

- Live in the present moment with your spouse and children wholeheartedly, minimizing worries about the future.
- Avoid dwelling on the past, a major source of stress, and instead focus on the present to make thoughtful decisions, fostering mental peace.
- Mindfulness reduces anxiety and contributes to a fulfilling life by enhancing your ability to appreciate the current moment.

Humility:

- Embrace humility to acknowledge both your strengths and weaknesses, fostering continuous growth and learning.
- Cultivate open-mindedness and effective communication, creating better relationships with your partner and family.
- Humility helps navigate life's challenges with grace, promoting understanding and harmony in relationships.

Sense of Purpose:

- Define and align your actions with a meaningful purpose, providing clear direction and motivation for life.
- Having a sense of purpose allows you to focus on what truly matters to you, fostering a meaningful and fulfilling life.
- It brings clarity to your goals and actions, contributing to a sense of fulfillment and satisfaction in your personal and family life.

BOTH PARTNERS SHOULD CREATE AN IMAGE OF A HAPPY FAMILY:

Standard of Living:

- We envision providing our children with a comfortable and secure standard of living, ensuring their basic needs are met while fostering an environment that encourages growth and exploration.

Dream House:

- We aspire to build a warm and welcoming home for our family, a place filled with love, laughter, and shared memories. It's a space where everyone feels safe, supported, and connected.

Financial and Moral Support:

- We commit to providing both financial and moral support to our children. This includes education, guidance, and encouragement to pursue their passions, fostering independence and resilience.

Balancing Responsibility and Fulfillment:

- We aim to balance our responsibilities effectively, ensuring that work and family commitments complement each other. Our goal is to lead a fulfilling life that prioritizes quality time with our loved ones.

Respect from Family and Society:

- We seek to earn respect from our family and society by upholding values of integrity, empathy, and kindness. Our actions will reflect our commitment to contributing positively to our community.

Financial Improvement Plan:

- We are following a well-thought-out financial plan, including budgeting, savings, and investments, to improve our financial condition steadily. This allows us to provide for our family's needs and future aspirations.

Setting an Example for Our Children:

- We engage in activities that set an excellent example for our son and daughter. This includes demonstrating the importance of hard work, resilience, and kindness. We encourage a love for learning, curiosity, and a sense of responsibility towards others.

BUILD A LEGACY FOR YOUR FAMILY'S FUTURE:

Generational trauma experienced by one generation has the potential to cast a long shadow, affecting subsequent generations. Trauma from the past is often passed down through stories, behaviors, and the social image of the family. Parents and grandparents who have endured trauma may unintentionally transmit their experiences to the younger generations.

The narratives and behaviors stemming from trauma can instill excessive fear or anxiety in their children, perpetuating a cycle of emotional distress.

The stories shared by family members vividly illustrate the consequences of past trauma, creating a sense of loss, anger, and distrust that carries on from generation to generation.

It is crucial to recognize that childhood, a critical stage of brain development, can be profoundly impacted by the lingering effects of generational trauma. The memories of trauma may create deep-seated emotional responses that influence the way individuals perceive the world and form relationships.

The formative years, marked by both positive and negative experiences, lay the foundation for children's emotional and physical health. These experiences significantly influence how they perceive the world and engage in communication and sharing. When aiming to break generational patterns, recognizing and understanding behavioral patterns becomes paramount.

If our present reflects the patterns of past generations, acknowledging these patterns is the crucial first step. Understanding the generational influences that shape behaviors and actively working to heal unwanted patterns become essential for creating a healthier and brighter future for both present and upcoming generations.

Children's behavior is a complex interplay of genetic factors, hormonal changes, and environmental influences. But just like the Hindi proverb: *"Jab Jago Tabhi Savera"*, it is never too late to mend someone or something.

Creating a healthy family system involves continuous effort and a commitment to nurturing harmonious relationships with your spouse, children, and parents. Demonstrating sensitivity towards each other within the family is essential, reflecting the responsibility and care you feel for your loved ones. The quality of our relationships is shaped by the thoughts and beliefs we hold.

Couples can start by mutually believing in their ability to create prosperity together. Recognizing that every thought and action contributes to shaping the future is crucial. Negative vibes within your home, often fueled by criticism, guilt, and fear, are reflective of inner thoughts. These negative thoughts often arise from self-blame or blaming others.

Clarification of mind becomes essential to address such challenges. Identify the thoughts that create problems in your life and raise awareness about your inner thoughts as the initial step in the healing process.

Sometimes, recurring behavioral patterns buried within us need acknowledgment and understanding for healing to occur. Such patterns resist change and can hinder personal growth, like:

Fear of Misunderstanding:

"My husband/wife won't understand my emotions."

Conflict with Upbringing:

"I cannot do this to support my wife; it goes against my upbringing."

THE HEALING PROCESS:

In many cases, the healing of a family is significantly influenced by the well-being of the mother. Women who struggle with unhealthy attachments, prioritizing their relationship with their husbands while neglecting their own well-being and identity, often experience feelings of abandonment and low self-esteem. They may depend heavily on their husbands for appreciation, approval, and social security, interpreting this dependency as love.

That's why women must cultivate interests beyond their immediate relationships to foster personal and emotional growth. By engaging in self-discovery and empowering themselves, women can develop a stronger sense of identity and independence.

So, identify the necessary changes for a better life and acknowledge the need for personal transformation.

Repeat the following affirmation in your mind: "I am willing to change my behavioral patterns that create a negative impact on my life and relationships." This repetition fosters awareness and provides clarity.

Shift away from a helpless attitude and focus on personal development. Appreciate your own efforts, foster confidence, and step out of the Blaming Zone. Loving yourself translates into a capacity to love your family genuinely, inspiring acts of sacrifice and compromise motivated by love rather than an emotional burden.

In the absence of love and sacrifices, compromises become emotional burdens, constraining the mind with negative thoughts and emotions. Embracing change, self-acceptance, and self-love form the pathway to a more fulfilling and positive life, influencing not only your well-being but also the dynamics within your family.

To protect your family from negative vibrations, consider these beautiful thoughts:

- **Control Your Mind:**
  - Success in life and a happy family requires control over your own mind. Direct your thoughts consciously towards positivity.
- **Focus on Purpose:**
  - The most practical method to control your mind is by focusing on the purpose of life. Align your thoughts and actions with meaningful goals.

- **Recognize Negative Influences:**
  - Identify negative influences in your life, whether self-created or from external sources. Awareness is the first step to positive change.
- **Close Your Mind to Negativity:**
  - Actively choose not to accept negativity. Close your mind to influences that hinder your well-being and family harmony.

REPEAT THESE AFFIRMATIONS TO CULTIVATE A POSITIVE MINDSET AND INFLUENCE YOUR EMOTIONAL WELL-BEING:

1. "I would like to find the negative emotion within me and correct it."
2. "I forgive and release the past. Now I am living in the present, looking forward to my prosperous future."
3. "I allow my thoughts to be free, discovering how wonderful my life is."
4. "I trust the process of life. I appreciate each moment and am ready to accept all life has to offer."
5. "I am taking right and good actions for my life. I release old patterns creating adverse conditions."
6. "I love myself. I am a loving person. I lovingly take care of my family."
7. "I easily leave habits that no longer contribute to my family's development."
8. "I lovingly forgive myself and those around me. I am willing to experience a happy life with my spouse and children."
9. "My children are safe and loved in my hands. They are welcomed and cherished in my family."

10. "I am free from irritation, guilt, and stress. I allow myself to flow with life and experience every moment."
11. "My family is well-structured and balanced. The divine spirit is the main structure of my family."
12. "I allow my spouse freedom and space. I am developing peace and harmony within and around me."
13. "I contribute to creating a loving and peaceful family life."
14. "The children in my family are divinely protected, surrounded by love and peace."
15. "I want to own my magnificent life with divine guidance. I seek forever."
16. "I've realized negative patterns and attracted wellness into my life."
17. "I make a habit to hear with calmness and speak with gentleness."
18. "I am motivating myself to bring peace to every corner of my life. I choose a peaceful and harmonious life."
19. "I allow the love from my heart to cleanse and heal every part of my life. I choose to support my family in a loving and joyous way."

Healing oneself is intricately tied to the healing of the family. Confronting negative thoughts and situations can be challenging, and awareness marks the initial step toward healing.

True healing unfolds when both husband and wife collaboratively dedicate themselves to the well-being of their family.

By working together, they create an environment that fosters growth, understanding, and resilience, contributing to the real healing of their lives and the collective strength of the family.

www.ingramcontent.com/pod-product-compliance
Lightning Source LLC
LaVergne TN
LVHW061557070526
838199LV00077B/7082